Changing Natures

DUCKWORTH DEBATES IN ARCHAEOLOGY

Series editor: Richard Hodges

Changing Natures

*Hunter-gatherers, first farmers
and the modern world*

Bill Finlayson
&
Graeme M. Warren

Duckworth

First published in 2010 by
Gerald Duckworth & Co. Ltd.
90-93 Cowcross Street, London EC1M 6BF
Tel: 020 7490 7300
Fax: 020 7490 0080
Info@duckworth-publishers.co.uk
www.ducknet.co.uk

A catalogue record for this book is available
from the British Library

ISBN 978-0-7156-3813-2

Typeset by Ray Davies

Contents

Acknowledgements

This book has arisen through a long process of dialogue between us and a great many colleagues – too many to name
individually here – who have been extremely generous with
their time, ideas and willingness to debate in formal and infor-
mal contexts. We thank them all and we hope they enjoy what
follows, even if they may not agree with all aspects of it. An
early draft of this book was read by Alan Barnard, Gabriel
Cooney, Bill Finlayson Snr, Nicky Milner, Garry Rollefson and
Caroline Wickham-Jones; we thank these readers for their very
valuable comments, critiques and suggestions for further work,
and we hope that this version is considered an improvement!
Needless to say, responsibility for any errors or misunderstandings in the pages that follow are ours alone.

We are grateful to the following colleagues for permission to
use illustrations: Alan Barnard, Seamas Caulfield and Conor
McDermott, Nigel Goring-Morris, Margaret Gowan & Co. Ltd.,
National Museum of the American Indian, Smithsonian Insti-
tution (photograph by Walter Larrimore), Gary Rollefson
(photographs by Peter Dorrell and Stuart Laidlaw), Rob Sands,
Klaus Schmidt and John Sunderland.

We are grateful to Duckworth, and in particular to Deborah
Blake, for support and patience during the production of this
book.

List of illustrations

7

Preface

As this book was nearing completion, one of us chanced upon a copy of *National Geographic* magazine (December 2009) lying in a waiting room. In it was an article by Michael Finkel focusing on the Hadza, a modern group of hunter-gatherers living in Tanzania in east Africa (Finkel 2009). In the article, Finkel quotes Frank Marlowe, a professor of anthropology from Florida State University who has worked with the Hadza since 1995, and who has stressed that the Hadza are not 'living fossils'. But Finkel appears to ignore this caveat, for the remainder of the article portrays the twenty-first-century hunter-gatherers of east Africa as a living representation of our pasts: 'Tanzania's hunter-gatherers live 10,000 years in the past'; and, in a description that features an interesting blurring of geography, genetics and insinuated antiquity of lifestyle: 'They live just south of the same section of the valley in which some of the oldest fossil evidence of early humans has been found. Genetic testing indicates that they may represent one of the primary roots of the human family tree – perhaps more than 100,000 years old.'

The Hadza are presented through a series of implicit comparisons with ourselves: they have no warfare and no infectious disease; they have no understanding of long periods of time or large numbers; they practise little or no ritual or ceremony (even in funerary contexts); they have few possessions, are egalitarian and have comparatively even gender roles; they have few social obligations, large amounts of leisure time, and are able to sleep whenever they wish; they live a life free of worry – with even their cooking style simple, and with-

9

out adornment. It is interesting to note that so many of these comparisons use a negative, an absence, to define the Hadza. The close descriptions of the hardships of a baboon hunt further the exoticizing of the Hadza, with feasting and celebration to follow; hands reaching into a baboon skull to scoop out and eat the stewed brain and, for the men only, communal bathing in a 'shallow muddy hole ... with lumps of cow manure floating about'.

The Hadza are presented by Finkel as demonstrating a radical alternative to the lifestyles of the modern Metropolitan readers of *National Geographic*; an 'other' to our stressed, conflicted, materially rich existence:

> There are things I envy about the Hadza – mostly, how free they appear to be. Free from possessions. Free of most social duties. Free from religious strictures. Free of many family responsibilities. Free from schedules, jobs, bosses, bills, traffic, taxes, laws, news, and money. Free from worry. Free to burp and fart without apology, to grab food and smoke and run shirtless through the thorns.

Yet Finkel is not simply suggesting that the Hadza's way of life constitutes a profound alternative to our metropolitan lifestyles, a different way of being. More significantly, he proposes that they are '... living a hunter-gatherer existence that is little changed from 10,000 years ago. What do they know that we've forgotten?' Thus the Hadza are not just portrayed as an example of a different way of living in the modern world; they are lifted out of our contemporary timeframe and made into a reminder of a hunter-gatherer past that we in the modern West have long left behind: 'What the Hadza appear to offer – and why they are of great interest to anthropologists – is a glimpse of what life may have been like before the birth of agriculture 10,000 years ago.' This collapsing of past and present renders the Hadza as without history, simply exemplars of what *we* once were (see also Fabian 1983). Finkel rightly stresses the problems that the Hadza face in maintaining their lifestyle in the twenty-first century, but is also very clear about the reason that hunter-gathers are now under such threat – the discovery of farming.

For more than 99 percent of the time since the genus *Homo* arose two million years ago, everyone lived as hunter-gatherers. Then, once plants and animals were domesticated, the discovery sparked a complete reorganization of the globe. Food production marched in lockstep with greater population densities, which allowed farm-based societies to displace or destroy hunter-gatherer groups. Villages were formed, then cities, then nations. And in a relatively brief period, the hunter-gatherer lifestyle was all but extinguished.

The discovery of farming is presented as the most significant change in human history – an origin point at which 'reorganization' takes pace, and our ancient, hunter-gatherer lifestyles were lost. The discovery of farming is also collapsed into the present, another key feature of much discourse which regards farming as modern behaviour.

Finkel's article is a classic example of a kind of discourse critiqued by the cultural theorist Edward Said. Said's 1978 book *Orientalism: Western Conceptions of the Orient* argued that there was an inescapable link between knowledge and power in forms of representation, and that the ways in which the West represented the Orient during the nineteenth and twentieth centuries in particular was directly linked to political relations of dominance. Europe's representations of the 'others' it encountered in the era of colonial expansion were not neutral. In fact through various media, Europe ' "constructs" and dominates Orientals in the process of knowing them' (Ashcroft & Ahluwalia 1999: 57). While on the one hand Western representations portrayed the Oriental other as exotic and attractive, at the same time the structure of the narrative served to marginalize those who were being described, often setting them aside from the march of history, and left to serve

11

as a timeless 'other' against which the colonial West could construct its own identities. Most importantly, the whole academic discourse that existed (and still exists) about the Orient is not, in a straightforward way, a discourse that simply tells us about the Orient; as Said argues ('Orientalism responded more to the culture that produced it, than to its putative object', 1978: 22), it tells us about ourselves.

It is not difficult to see how Finkel's account is classically Orientalist: his narrative is exoticizing and at times eroticizing – for example when a teenage boy and young woman move away from the party and 'sneak into the bush' – but it also marginalizes and disempowers; with these hunter-gatherers on the periphery of the dominant global process – the expansion of agriculture. Even more clearly, his representation of the Hadza (his 'putative object') tells us as much about the concerns of the metropolitan West (the 'culture that produced' his account) as it does about the Hadza.

Finkel's article is, of course, a piece of journalism, not an academic paper. But he does capture a series of profoundly important stereotypes about how hunter-gatherers live and how they may in some way represent our past. Finkel's wording provides a vivid example of the relationships between representations of hunter-gatherers, first farmers and the modern world. This book is about how our understandings of the nature of hunter-gather societies have influenced our descriptions of the first use of domesticated plants and animals. We will suggest that much of what has been said about hunter-gatherers and the first farmers can be shown to reflect our attitudes to the modern world and that, at times, this has stopped us from gaining a full appreciation of human diversity in the past.

Introduction

'Prehistory' ... refers to the lives of our first hunter-gatherer ancestors, and then to those early times when humans, through the development of agriculture, were able to turn away from a life of hunting and gathering and to live in villages and then in towns. (Renfrew 2007: vii-viii)

This book is about one of the most important and most often discussed processes in prehistory, the adoption of agriculture. As the transition from dependence on wild food resources, to production by domestication and cultivation, it was one of the most important stages in human development. It is frequently associated with the origins of other changes, such as the beginnings of organized religion, urbanization, specialization of labour, or even more generally the emergence of truly modern humans. Our central contention is that the usual narratives about such matters rely on stereotypes and simplistic notions of who hunter-gatherers and farmers really were, and still are, and that the narratives themselves are best understood as reflections of how we perceive our place in modern, predominantly urban society. We compare early prehistoric rural people with modern urban ones, as this is the contrast that is drawn upon in our imaginations.

Archaeologists have long argued that their key contribution to learning is to examine changes in human societies over the long term, in contrast to the shorter perspectives of ethnography or historical analysis. Moreover, they work explicitly or implicitly within a broad framework of social evolution (cf.

13

Pluciennik 2005). This includes a multitude of concepts, but its central idea is that the organization of human societies has changed over time, usually with an implication of 'progress'. Traditionally, we have divided the past into stages, either those of cultural evolution (savagery, barbarism, civilization), or those of the three-age archaeological system (Stone, Bronze and Iron Ages, each with many subdivisions). Attention has mainly been concentrated on the points of change between these divisions, on the supposition that within them change either does not happen, or does so very slowly. This system of division is now often seen as simply a convenient set of labels. There is increasing recognition that change is continuous, and that both change and stability are the result of constant renegotiation of the factors that control them. Nevertheless, the study of transitions remains a central focus of archaeological research.

The change from prehistoric people surviving on wild resources to modern ones living in sprawling cities, dependent on intensive industrialized agriculture, is an enormous one, and we do not seek to downplay this distinction. The more recent part of the process, in historic times, has long been spoken of as including an 'industrial revolution'. In the first half of the twentieth century Vere Gordon Childe took up this idea, and suggested that there had been a 'Neolithic revolution' of similar if not greater historical significance, which had separated hunter-gatherers and farmers. 'The escape from the impasse of savagery was an economic and scientific revolution that made the participants active partners with nature instead of parasites on nature' (Childe 1964: 55). Childe successfully welded together the general cultural stages of savagery, barbarism and civilization, developed in the North American anthropological tradition (Morgan 1877) with the European three-age system, based more specifically on material culture. He did so in an explicitly political context, and we will return to discuss this point at the close of our argument. While much has changed since then, and while many would disagree with the concept of an actual Neolithic revolution, some of Childe's basic ideas still underpin many debates today. Indeed, 'revolutions' continue to figure largely in new work. Many now talk of a 'symbolic revolution' (e.g. Cauvin 2000), while even more recently the 'agricultural revolution' has been reintroduced, albeit as a process extended both chronologically and spatially (cf. Barker 2006). For our present discussion, the biggest issue is the idea that there is an enormous gulf between those who farm, and those who do not. That hunter-gatherers are essentially different from farmers and that their ways of life are incompatible or opposed to one another has remained a central, fundamental plank of much archaeological debate. This question has become all the more important following recent suggestions by several scholars, most notably Colin Renfrew (2003) and Trevor Watkins (2004), that people do not really become fully human until the Neolithic, as it is only at this stage that the full human potentials for complexity are realized (see below for detail). If we follow these arguments, we either have to accept that contemporary or near-contemporary hunter-gatherers are not human, or that they have been made human by later contact with farmers. In any case, the implication is that pre-Neolithic revolution societies were something completely different, connected by subsistence perhaps with hunter-gatherers today, but not actually *human* societies in the way that we are.

As we will demonstrate, one of the key functions of the concept of the hunter-gatherer, historically, has been to set up an 'other' against which we can define our modern selves. It is therefore no surprise that a logical outcome of its use in discussing the Neolithic revolution is to assume that hunter-gatherers were not at all like us. We reject the arguments of Renfrew and Watkins entirely, and we argue that people have been fully human for much longer than the ideas of these authors imply. However, and importantly, such acceptance still does not automatically lead to the recognition of any culture or society as having standard, common hunter-gatherer features over long periods. Instead, we can consider more recent anthropological models, which see hunter-gatherer societies as extremely diverse and flexible, having significant overlap with 'horticultural' ones. Modern or recent hunter-gatherers have the same kind of basis as other small-scale societies, and it is one that is seen increasingly as a conceptual one rather than being tied to their means of subsistence (cf. Bird-David 1990). The nature of pre-Neolithic societies and the use of the term hunter-gatherer to describe them have yet to be established from archaeological evidence, and we will consider the extensive use of analogies on which many models depend.

Discussions about the historical significance of the Neolithic revolution or transition are discussions about the evolution of the human species and the defining features of that species. Cultural evolution as an overall concept has become associated with *progress* over time: 'the idea that evolution is a steady, linear upwards movement, a single inexorable process of improvement, leading ... "from gas to genius" and beyond ...' (Midgley 2002: 7). On this view, the agricultural revolution might be seen as marking an important point on the route from simplicity to complexity, from them to us. Despite the common belief that hunter-gatherers might be opposed to farming, and indeed might be happy with their own way of life, it appears to remain central to much archaeological thought that the transition to farming is an upward step, a threshold to be crossed, a mark of success. We will consider this point further when we look at the history and definition of hunter-gatherers, but for now we can make the connection between 'progress' and a teleological model of history which sees the past in terms of a stream of events that lead to Western civilization. It has an underlying framework within which we can trace a chain of development, in which people gradually collect the necessary building-blocks of Western civilization, and then retain each of them as part of the emerging package. Post-modern calls for alternative histories have had little impact on the study of the transition of hunter-gatherers to farmers. And yet it was made clear right from the start, by Childe himself, that this understanding of our historical focus is subjective in its nature. As he noted, 'If our own culture can claim to be in the main stream, it is only because our cultural tradition has captured and made tributary a larger volume of once parallel traditions' (Childe 1964: 29). In any case, biological evolutionary theory does not support progress over time. One recent review (Sterelny & Griffiths 1999: 284) states that 'the idea that evolution is progressive is particularly problematic both conceptually and empirically'. Instead of implying increasing progress, evolution over time is best understood as leading to increased variability. The relationship between variability and complexity is more problematic, and Sterelny and Griffiths note that 'an evolution of evolvability' (pp. 286-7), has led to a increase over time in the possible average complexity in existence. The evolution of evolvability implies a new evolutionary mechanism, such as when the invention of the organism, as opposed to single eukaryotic cells, created new possibilities for complexity across the biological system as a whole. This should not, however, be confused with necessarily implying a directional movement to complexity (progress) for any individual species.

One of our central contentions, then, is that the common model of agricultural revolutions as fundamental shifts in human history is founded upon, and perpetuates, a radical over-simplification of the possibilities for human diversity: it is at odds, not only with many of the archaeological findings that we discuss, but also with accepted evolutionary theory. In contrast to the epigraph with which we opened this Introduction, which represents a generally held view, we prefer to emphasize *variability,* rather than any supposed march of *progress.*

Possibly because the transition from hunting and gathering to agriculture is understood as a global evolutionary shift, it is often seen as requiring, or being suited to, some general explanation that 'should be plausible, simple, causal, verifiable, and global' (Price & Gebauer 1995: 6). It is frequently the subject of large-scale synthetic works in which, at times, the detail of the model overrides the available archaeological evidence. In this book we make no pretence that we will cover all the data in detail, and we are not attempting to create a new globe-spanning history. An aspect of our work which we hope will emerge is the importance of working with specific examples, and developing local histories, rather than cherry-picking data in order to produce synthetic models.

A belief that the transition to the Neolithic was a very significant or key stage in the development of modern Western civilization is often used as a reason for studying it closely. However, the perceived importance of farming may be based more upon its importance *now* than on its significance *then*. The perceived difference in life-style relates more to farmers in the present or in the relatively recent past, rather than having anything to do with the lives of prehistoric people (as seen in the example from Finkel above, where the discovery of farming is very much part of the *now*). It is now recognized that at least some aspects of the transition may have occurred over very extended periods, which makes the term 'revolution' less appropriate, but the change is still seen to be enormous, and as having broken through Childe's 'impasse'. It is therefore thought to have been revolutionary in magnitude if not in rapidity (e.g. Lewis-Williams & Pearce 2005). Revolution therefore *appears to be a necessary concept* (e.g. Gamble 2007) to get us from 'other' to 'us', non-human to human, hunter-gatherer to peasant farmer, but these are all categories we have imposed on the data, possibly creating sharp divisions where there were none in reality.

Revolutions and notions of progress through time are also permeated by religious ideas. Smail believes that religious conceptions of time and space underpin many general historical narratives and that in the twentieth century the origins of agriculture replaced the Biblical chronology: 'The sacred was deftly translated into a secular key: the Garden of Eden became the irrigated fields of Mesopotamia, and the creation of man was reconfigured as the rise of civilization' (Smail 2007: 4, 12-39). Discussion of revolution also highlights distinctions made between 'natural' evolution and 'cultural' evolution. These can be seen as attempts to define the point at which biology is separated from history, and humans from the rest of life on earth (Ingold 2000: 184-5). Smail (2007: 2-3) suggests

18

1. Reconstructions at PPNB Beidha, Jordan, being used to film a documentary for *National Geographic*. Despite the serious intent of the filming, the actors are dressed as primitive savages.

that prehistory itself operates as a 'buffer zone', maintaining a distinction between a period characterized by the biological evolution of hominids and one characterized by historical processes. Such a buffer zone, a time without change, necessitates the appearance of revolutions to effect change (Fig. 1 shows how strong the idea of the primitive savage is in our imagination). This, in turn, can be seen as connected to the catastrophist paradigm of historical writing, where resetting events can allow histories to begin 'in the middle' (Smail 2007: 21) following an event; with the Biblical Deluge providing the prime example (see also Freeman 2004: 163-89).

> The Neolithic Rubicon performs a narrative function eerily similar to the Viconian Deluge. There are some obvious differences. The Deluge was a resetting event ... The Neolithic Rubicon was a passage from stasis to progress. But both sit astride the buffer zone between non-history and history. Both act as a rupture ... . (Smail 2007: 37)

In all this it is important to note that the presentation of hunter-gatherers as the natural state of humans, at their point of origin, and separated from us by revolutions, assumes that they are influenced only by 'natural' (biological) processes, whereas farmers are 'historical' beings, and are therefore fundamentally different in character. The obvious political implications are discussed below.

Social evolutionary typologies encourage reliance on a model of historic change by distinct stages, brought about by revolutions. The need for histories punctuated by revolutions, or of cultural evolution between different kinds of human societies, presupposes the existence of *categories*.. For this book, the most fundamental of these are hunting and gathering, and farming. We have used these concepts so far, throughout this introduction, with little or no definition. We assume that they are familiar, and that most of our readers will accept, for example, that for most of human history people survived by hunting and gathering, before the relatively recent appearance of farming. This understanding appears so obvious that it is rarely even considered, yet, as we shall explore below, the actual concept of the hunter-gatherer is a relatively modern one and is much more complicated than might be supposed. There is a difference between the simple notion that people used to subsist on wild, or natural resources, and the much debated and analysed category of 'hunter-gatherer'. Unfortunately, this difference is rarely questioned or even recognized in the study of prehistory, and models of contemporary hunter-gatherer societies are imported wholesale into the deep past, advancing neither our understanding of that past nor of hunter-gatherers in general, but simply imposing the ethnographic present onto our often scanty archaeological evidence.

In consequence, we believe that to understand the transitions that most certainly did occur, we need to unpack the idea of hunter-gatherer, especially as it is applied to prehistory, and the idea of farmer as it is applied to early developments in food production. This unpacking inevitably brings about a need to reconsider some of the other baggage that comes with these concepts, ideas regarding simple egalitarian societies, the concept of the village, and finally, what we mean by the Neolithic. This is a tall order. To supply answers within the covers of this book we will be making some broad statements, which we will then illustrate with case studies. Fig. 2 provides a general timeline of the periods to be discussed. Our aim is to

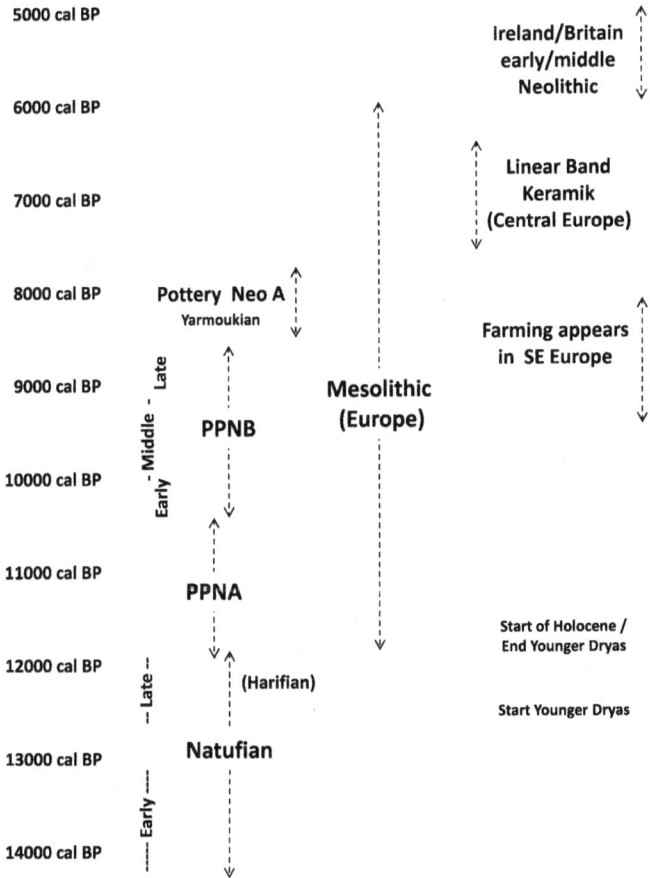

2. Main time periods discussed in the text. Periods are presented separately for ease of identification but in many instances clearly developed from their immediate predecessors.

prompt debate on matters that we consider to have been over-looked or misunderstood.

The structure of this book

The question 'what is a hunter-gatherer' is indeed a deceptively easy one. The term is often not defined, or it is simply assumed to mean a reliance on wild, as opposed to domesticated, re-sources. As we shall discuss, the concept is a recent one, based on the study of contemporary or near contemporary societies. Powerful popular stereotypes are evoked, which have a prob-lematical relationship to realities past and present. In Chap-ters 1 and 2 we explore some of the issues raised in an archaeological context. Chapter 1 discusses the background and general use of the term, before focusing on the particular issue of hunter-gatherer *diversity* in present-day societies. This in turn leads on to the problems of how this diversity has been reduced into simple stereotypes in many archaeological narra-tives, and of the uncritical use of modern hunter-gatherers as a point of comparison with archaeological examples.

In Chapter 2 we explore the ways in which the use of these labels – hunter-gatherer, farmer, prehistoric, present – serve particular modern political ends. We begin by asking what the world would look like without the concept of 'hunter-gatherer', before we move on to the way in which hunting and gathering life-styles are represented in the context of green politics. We then examine the ways in which some Irish archaeological texts have presented the relations between hunter-gatherers, the land of Ireland, and its history, before casting a critical eye on reconstruction drawings – as further examples of repre-sentations that tell us more about the modern world than about the prehistoric past. We end the chapter by suggesting that if both hunter-gatherers and farmers are very diverse groups, we should be looking at a range of different possible forms of social organization, rather than just providing simplistic labels.

The association between farming and a settled way of life is very strong. In Chapter 3 we examine its relationship to the rather romantic picture of farmers living in villages, which colours much archaeological interpretation, and which also plays a central part in accounts of the differences between hunter-gatherers and farmers. Even where we can see a long history of generally increasing sedentism at this time, as in southwest Asia, we need to exercise some caution in accepting ideas about village life, and even more so with respect to ideas about early urbanization. Elsewhere, in both the archaeological record and in contemporary ethnography, we can see greatly varying patterns of settlement associated with farming.

Chapter 4 examines the association between agriculture and social hierarchy, concentrating on the common supposition that hunter-gatherers are egalitarian and that the Neolithic revolution led to a move away from this origin-point. This in turn leads to a consideration of the contradictory roles sometimes ascribed to non-egalitarian hunter-gatherers. We conclude by discussing the selective use of data in the construction of 'origins' narratives.

Chapter 5 gives examples of recent models which propose that people do not become fully human until the Neolithic revolution. This argument, which in some sense has provided our motive for writing this book, is considered in detail. We discuss first the so-called 'cognitive revolution' that is supposed by some writers to have taken place with the coming of the Neolithic – and which they have promoted as being distinct from, and more important than, the 'human revolution' associated with the evolution of modern humans. We then deal with the related perception that the origins of religion lay in this period.

Chapter 6 concludes the book by reaffirming our commitment to understanding how the varied forms of human society were created in the past. We discuss again the need to avoid using mere archaeological labels in place of real explanations. We suggest that 'tipping points' may be a useful concept in considering the nature of changes over time. We stress the need to concentrate our attention on the details of human history and not to move on to global models by brushing aside the complexity of the data.

1

What is a hunter-gatherer?

The field of hunter-gathering studies has been a conten-
tious brand of anthropology since its inception two
centuries ago. (Guenther 2007: 371)

It is commonly stated that humans have lived as hunter-gatherers for a vast proportion of their evolutionary history. Different accounts may give the figure as 90%, or 99%, but the
general impression is clear – that hunting and gathering life-
styles are the basic human condition. The idea of a long deep
history, where little changed, allows for the appearance of
agriculture to be seen as a revolutionary change in the nature
of humanity, but also begs a simple but very important question: what *is* a 'hunter-gatherer'? And following on from this,
what is it supposed to *signify,* that so much of human history is
that of hunter-gatherers?

The modernity of hunter-gatherers

The origins of the term 'hunter-gatherer' are associated with
the colonial expansion of European nation states and the ways
in which their encounters with different ways of life were
systematized into broad frameworks for understanding human
diversity. Conceptions of differences between groups of people
had, of course, existed before the development of the notion of
hunter-gatherer societies, but these were not directly constructed around the subsistence basis of societies. Thomas
Hobbes's famous definition of the 'Naturall Condition of Man-
kind' as 'the life of man, solitary, poore, nasty, brutish, and

short' (1651) is not a description of hunter-gatherers, but a statement about the distinction between the natural and the civilized. Related discussions, but with very different emphases, held up the 'noble savage' as a contrast to the excesses of Western urban society.

In fact, the development of this conception of hunting and gathering societies, and the use of the subsistence base as a criterion for definition, is particularly associated with eighteenth-century social thought, and in particular with the Scottish moral philosophy of this period. Barnard (2004: 31) claims that hunting and gathering societies were 'an eighteenth-century Scottish invention'. He refers to a series of discussions associated with the contemporary definition of property rights, and related theories, by philosophers and economists of the Enlightenment. He says that Hobbes and Locke may have had the idea of hunter-gatherers, but that because their concept of society was political, they believed that such hunter-gatherers were pre-society. The Scottish concept, on the other hand, was an economic one. Barnard still believes (pers. comm.) that there is a difference between a society-less hunter-gatherer and a member of a hunter-gatherer society.

One must also consider the association between the Judaeo-Christian understanding that change is directional over time, and the notion of *progress*. Within this framework hunter-gatherers could form an origin point for the development of property rights and territory in the modern world. Here, as elsewhere, the notion of hunter-gatherers was vital to the definition of what it was to be, *not a hunter-gatherer,* but something else. This transition was the point from which the history began that led to the modern West.

In the early and middle twentieth century, similar concepts continued to be used, although now within the nascent discipline of anthropology. Formal social evolutionary models became increasingly important, and one influential scheme (Service 1962) was formulated which proposed a succession of different forms of social organization, proceeding from bands, to tribes, to chiefdoms, to states. Bands, the base of this trajectory, were supposed to be composed of small groups of people – a magic number of 25 is sometimes proposed. Their members had no fixed social roles or hierarchy, and each band comprised a loose and sometimes temporary alliance of nuclear families. Hunting-gathering and social organization in bands were (and still are) seen as more or less universally concomitant in such models. In 1966 a conference on *Man the Hunter* was hosted in Chicago (Lee & Devore 1968). This marked a watershed in hunter-gatherer studies, and reflected an increasing engagement with hunting and gathering societies from a variety of theoretical viewpoints. One of the most influential of these views came from Marshall Sahlins (1972: 1-39), who suggested that rather than emphasizing that hunter-gatherers had few *possessions*, and were therefore poor, an alternative was to recognize that these societies limited their *needs*. When they had enough material possessions to fulfil their needs they could not be seen as being poor. Sahlins also presented data suggesting that hunter-gatherers had to work very few hours each day to obtain their subsistence requirements. Far from being a life of miserable labour and few rewards, this was the 'original affluent society', which Sahlins described as a Zen alternative to modern lifestyles (the parallels with the article by Finkel, reviewed in our Preface, are clear). Clearly resonant in the wider social milieu of the late 60s and early 70s, such models were combined with general post-colonial trends in intellectual and political thought, and led to a significant increase in interest in hunter-gatherer societies past and present, both within and beyond academia. Given the significance accorded to the idea of the 'original affluent society' in perceptions of hunter-gatherers, especially among prehistoric archaeologists, it is important to note that many aspects of Sahlins's model have since been criticized, and that arguably he was just using hunter-gatherers to make a modern political point.

Since that time, there have been diverse hunter-gatherer studies in archaeology and anthropology, with contributions from across the globe, and a multiplicity of different theoretical perspectives. Varied attempts have been made to characterize the field, encompassing evolutionary models, ecological models, symbolic approaches, gender approaches – including the riposte of *Woman the Gatherer* to *Man the Hunter* (Dahlberg 1983). However, the dynamism of the debate, and the fact that many contributions cut across fields of interest, means that such classifications are difficult. Most recently there has been a significant emphasis on the importance of indigenous representation in organized debates about hunter-gatherers, not least in the context of the social, political and economic marginalization of these groups in the twentieth century (see below). The relationships between hunter-gatherers and other groups have also come under discussion. This is a topic of considerable significance for the use in archaeology of modern hunter-gatherers to provide approximate pictures of their prehistoric equivalents.

A major area of research in recent years has been concerned with the importance of historical context in the study of present-day hunting and gathering peoples. It is especially significant for developing a better understanding of hunter-gatherer diversity and flexibility. As this interest in the history of hunter-gatherer societies developed, it led to a revisionist approach, which contended that modern hunter-gatherers are not pristine survivals from the Stone Age, nor are they to be separated from wider political and historical developments. For the revisionists, the view of hunter-gatherers as survivors from the past was a romantic fabrication (see, e.g., Wilmsen 1983). Mathias Guenther (2007: 376) wrote: 'The revisionist view regards extant hunter-gatherers not as cultural aboriginals but as social marginals, tied in different forms of dependency relationships to regional agropastoralist state societies, or to the colonialist, postcolonialist, or capitalist world system'. The debate within anthropology was fierce, as it raised fundamental questions about contemporary hunter-gatherer social and political organization. However, although the revisionist view was acknowledged in some archaeological quarters (for example Shott 1992) and although many of the protagonists were archaeologists and historians, it has had relatively little impact in research on the Eurasian origins of the Neolithic.

1. What is a hunter-gatherer?

This history of the concept of hunter-gatherers has to be regrettably brief, but we hope we have made it clear that the *concept* of hunting-gathering has its own historical context, that it has developed in particular ways, that this development has come from specific recent or present-day contexts, and that it has always been related to the way the matter has been understood in the modern Western world. We will return to some of these issues in the following chapter, providing case studies to show how these concepts were used, or not used, in order to buttress particular twentieth-century senses of identity. At this stage, however, we have mainly just suggested that the answer to our original question, 'what is a hunter-gatherer?' is not as simple as it might have seemed. We now turn our attention to the characteristics of hunting and gathering societies in the modern world.

Overall diversity

It is clear that the number of today's hunting and gathering societies is only a small fraction of the number of those that existed in the past. For some of the more recent of them we have records describing the ways in which they lived, their understanding of the world, or the foods they relied upon. Some of these accounts date back to the period of colonial contact, or missionary activity, and some are the result of detailed anthropological study. It is impossible to provide a definitive number for those that have been studied. *The Cambridge Encyclopaedia of Hunter-Gatherers* (Lee & Daly (eds) 1999: 12) does not attempt to be comprehensive. It includes 'over fifty of the world's best documented groups', with examples drawn from many areas across the globe. However, there are many parts of the world where farmers have long since displaced hunter-gatherers, for example Europe, or much of continental Asia. Our modern sample is geographically biased towards agriculturally marginal lands – this is one of the problems of using modern hunter-gatherers as analogues for past ones. We will return to this issue in the final part of this chapter.

Most recent anthropological accounts of hunter-gatherers place a heavy emphasis on *diversity*, but this feature is not always immediately apparent in the archaeological literature. The question is left open regarding how much hunter-gatherers, as a category, have in common. It is very difficult to find concise definitions, and most are surrounded by caveats of various kinds. It is also only fair to note that, in keeping with our main thesis, we will not attempt to provide our own definition! Lee and Daly's introduction to the Cambridge encyclopaedia includes a definition that runs to three pages, followed by a further page for divergences (Lee & Daly 1999: 3-6). They say that definitions must be multi-faceted, to include aspects of subsistence, social organization and world-view or cosmology. 'Subsistence' requires a reliance on wild food, with no domesticated kinds, but in fact, ambiguity arises even here, early on in our definitions, since many hunter-gatherers have domesticated the dog, and some resource-management practices are strategies that give rise to domestication, rather than being wholly distinct. Social organization for *most* is in *bands*, they are *relatively* egalitarian, *tend* to be mobile, and *almost all* have common property. As to their world view, stress is put on an ethos of sharing, and the cosmological significance of an animate and giving environment. Areas of divergence include the extent and character of interpersonal violence, the nature of gender relations, and the sexual division of labour, as well as broader issues of organization (see below for a discussion of 'complex' hunter-gatherers). Some discussions (for example Lee & Daly 1999, Guenther 1999) imply that hunter-gatherer cosmology can be generically described as Shamanistic, a term derived from Siberian ethnography and referring to ritual specialists who utilize trance states to mediate the human and spirit worlds. Others have suggested that the extension of this terminology from northern Eurasia is not appropriate (McCall 2007, with further references), and that important differences exist between superficially similar ritual practices, past or present.

Any general statements about what hunter-gatherers are, caveats notwithstanding, conceal considerable ambiguities and diversity. Take the seemingly simple statement that hunter-gatherers are mobile. Robert Kelly's *Foraging Spectrum* (1995), for example, includes data on the number of times that various hunter-gatherer groups practise 'residential mobility' (move their home base) each year, as well as on the average distance of these moves. We can give here some of the annual extremes: groups such as the Baffinland Inuit practise residential mobility 60 times, averaging 12 km. The Nunamiut of Alaska, who live at a similar latitude, move 10 times, averaging 69.5 km. The Ngadadjara of the Australian desert move 37 times, averaging 43 km. Many groups do not exhibit residential mobility at all, but practise 'logistical mobility', sending task groups out from their base camps to short-term ones: the Ainu of Hokkaido spend 48 days a year on such trips, the Aleut of Alaska 32 days. Many groups within a given society practise combinations of these strategies (for further discussion of residential and logistical mobility, see Binford 1980). It can be seen that there is considerable diversity in the degree and nature of mobility, and although there are some very general rules – for example, hunter-gatherers in deserts and in the high Arctic tend to move a lot – there are exceptions even to most of these generalizations.

Moreover, it is important to recall that farming communities and industrial societies – which together provide the 'settled' contrast to our mobile hunter-gatherers – may also be highly mobile. One of us (GW) travels 80 km a day commuting to work while the other (BF) faces a much shorter daily commute from home to office, but is frequently on the move between Jordan and the UK. Both of us have moved from the areas where we grew up. Such mobility is, of course, not unusual in a globalized twenty-first-century economy, and it does make one wonder why we should stress mobility as such a key characteristic of hunter-gatherers. Hugh Brody (2001) has made the provocative argument that in a long-term perspective it is the land-hungry agriculturalists who are mobile, always expanding and seeking new lands to exploit, while hunter-gatherers tend to stay in one place and have very strong links to it. Many pastoral or swidden agriculturalists also cover considerable distances in the course of their routine subsistence practices. Our definitions of mobile and settled are more slippery than we might suppose and, in this instance, there may also be the suggestion of a historical political agenda. By defining hunter-gatherers as mobile, not settled, transitory and not fixed, they can be embedded into nature, set apart from history – simply part of the rhythms and routines of nature's seasonal changes. Given the colonial background to most encounters with hunter-gatherers, their ultimate dispossession by farmers was facilitated by a concept that they were mobile, and sub-sequently did not really settle a landscape, which was therefore available for agriculture.

Thus, even a general statement that hunter-gatherers tend to be mobile raises significant questions, and can be perceived as having arisen in a particular social situation. It is hard to see how a definition that incorporates such a statement can allow us to say anything significant about the human past. And as noted above, and discussed in more detail below, the present-day sample of hunting and gathering societies is small, and comes from a particular subset of mostly marginal environments. Diversity in the past is likely to have been even greater.

It would be easy to see this discussion as simply academic wrangling, with a counter-example being cited for every proposed rule. However, questions of general rules and specific examples are of real importance to archaeological practice. Archaeology is always a comparative exercise. We attempt to understand what we do not know – the past – by reference to what we do know – the present. When we describe an ancient building as a 'house' we do so by comparison with our common-sense notion that there are buildings in which people live and which we call houses. Our models of hunter-gatherer society in the present or near present inevitably form the bases of our understanding of hunter-gatherers in the past. Sometimes the comparison is made explicitly, at other times it is not. In either case what we are doing is forming an analogy, and the nature of our analogical reasoning is a theme that runs throughout this book. Archaeology offers us a chance to demonstrate the diversity of ways of being human, whereas the use of unsupportably strict general rules runs the risk of writing particular models of the present into the past. This risk is especially high when the general rules take the form of implicit, common-sense assumptions.

Hunter-gatherer stereotypes

We can see that extremely variable present-day societies are allocated to the hunter-gatherer category. Nevertheless, their assumed primitive nature, and the stage they are taken to have reached in evolutionary models, have made them a rich source of analogies with the archaeological remains of societies that lived before farming began. Traditional archaeological models have been dominated by ideas of progress and development within social evolutionary frameworks, and the archaeological perspective on hunter-gatherers has been created to suit this framework. As Guenther (2007) has observed, it is by a strange twist that past hunter-gatherers are seen to have a trajectory of historical change, while the equivalent of fossil evidence is provided by present-day ones, supposedly static. This perspective has not been easily arrived at, since most of the past hunter-gatherer societies are also seen in the archaeological literature as being themselves incapable of initiating developmental change, and requiring external stimuli, such as climate change, to produce it.

To enable interpretations of change to be made among hunter-gatherers, archaeologists have been enthusiastic in accepting a model in which the diversity of recent or present-day societies subsumed into this category is divided into two generalized and stereotypical forms. The first of these is the so-called 'simple hunter-gatherer'. The San of the Kalahari desert (see Fig. 3), and the Aboriginals of Australia provide archetypes. Typically these societies are seen as highly mobile, with limited material culture, no storage of foods, but with a strategy of subsisting on what can be caught or gathered on a daily basis, with much smaller populations than could be sustained in their environment, living in egalitarian groups that practise an easy sharing of resources. These are the societies referred to as the 'original affluent society', with few wants which are all satisfied. The apparent simplicity of their societies has led to the assumption that they represent an essential way of human life that predates all later developments, most particularly the development of farming. As such, they often form the basis for discussions of all human societies before about 10,000 years ago. Furthermore, a key aspect of this stereotype is that it can be seen to be entirely different from farming societies in almost every respect – mobile, reliant on wild resources, small-scale, egalitarian, and so on. 'Simple' hunter-gatherers form the standard model of what a hunter-gatherer should be, not least in the popular imagination, and all too frequently in archaeological expectations. It is still common to find archaeological essays at introductory university level extensively populated by the simple hunter-gatherer stereotype, often associated with words such as primitive and savage.

The second stereotype is the 'complex hunter-gatherer'. The models were originally based on the societies of the northwest coast of North America, which had developed their economies with significant input from predictable and enormous runs of salmon. This economic base has been seen as enabling them to organize themselves in ways entirely different from those of 'simple' hunter-gathering, in that they are increasingly sedentary, produce and store surpluses, and have emerging hierarchies. Archaeological models grant them some ability to initiate change. Direct comparisons have been made between these societies and Mesolithic societies of the early Holocene in northwest Europe, especially the Ertebølle of southern Scandinavia, as well as with late Pleistocene societies of southwest Asia, especially the Natufian. We will discuss these examples in detail in Chapter 4, but it is important to note here that they are apparently being used in partially contradictory ways in these contexts. In general, complex hunter-gatherers appear rarely in anthropological literature, but have been identified

1. What is a hunter-gatherer?

3. Naro (Nharo) band on the move, by donkey, 1975. The Naro are San hunter-gatherers in Western Botswana. Here they use a domesticated animal to help in routine mobility.

more commonly in archaeological research, especially in the late Pleistocene and early Holocene (see, e.g., Price & Brown (eds) 1985). It is also worth noting that although one may discuss simple and complex hunter-gatherers, it is very unusual to hear any discussion of simple and complex *farmers*: the assumption of complexity is built in.

There are basic problems with these categories and the way in which they are deployed. The first and most fundamental one is the assumption that present-day hunter-gatherers form a good analogy for societies that existed more than 10,000 years ago. We will return to this important point.

The second problem is related to this first one, and also to the idea that simple hunter-gatherers are in any real way 'simple' and therefore possibly 'original'. The idea of 'original' turns us once again to ideas of the noble savage living in the golden age, or life in the Garden of Eden. Tilley, for example, argues that the late Mesolithic communities of southern Scandinavia might be described as living in 'primitive communism … I am politically old-fashioned enough even to want to describe it as a Garden of Eden before the Fall' (Tilley 1996: 68). Because such societies are, to such a large extent, defined by what they *do not* have, it also allows analogies to be made which assume that the characteristics of such societies are ancient, and that they form the base-line from which everything else develops. This requires an assumption that contemporary hunter-gatherers are unchanging and timeless – that they have not developed from the original state. The 10,000 years that separate modern hunter-gatherers from the past must have encompassed a monumental lack of change! By being discovered, hunter-gatherers have become part of modern, global, colonial and imperial systems (Layton 2001) and they cannot be divorced from these contexts. Hunter-gatherers have their own history.

The third problem is that to reduce hunter-gatherers into two such generalized forms does not reflect the diversity that clearly exists, and existed, within different societies. It has been noted that archaeologists tend to identify complex hunter-gatherers far more readily than anthropologists do. This should not surprise us. Complex hunter-gathering is seen as a necessary stage on the developmental path to farming. Simple hunter-gatherers are too sharply opposed to a farming way of life to be conceived of as being able to make the transition. Complex hunter-gatherers are seen as opposed to the simple hunter-gathering way of life, and therefore as providing a suitable evolutionary platform for farming – although an opposition between complex hunter-gatherers and farmers is also posited, so as to allow them to resist farming, in northwest Europe. To explain change, these contradictory patterns of amenability or opposition require a language of major revolutions, and large steps to be taken on an evolutionary ladder.

1. What is a hunter-gatherer?

Unfortunately, if we set up a dichotomous model of simple and complex hunter-gatherers to escape from the apparent impossibility of unchanging hunter-gatherers developing farming, we just move the problem back a step – we now have to show how simple could become complex.

The division into these two generalized forms causes a further problem, which we will discuss in detail when we consider farming societies, as it concerns the way in which many 'simple' societies are involved in activities that relate to our conventional idea of farming, including those which have adopted strategies to preserve or enhance the yield from gathering sites, and even some which have adopted cultivation. Bird-David (1999) notes that the there is is a considerable overlap between foraging and agricultural activities in south Asia, making it hard to classify people who practise both, and thereby excluding them from many discussions. In parts of south America, southeast Asia, and Australia, there are 'simple' hunter gatherer societies that practice cultivation.

Stereotypes rely on a set of characteristics that supposedly always go together, combining the degree of residential permanence with social structure and economy. This perception goes against everything we know about hunter-gatherer diversity, but it appears to be a very useful pragmatic tool for archaeologists – the moment we can identify sedentism, we can claim to be able to deduce hierarchy, and so on. Unfortunately, such a neat association is not borne out by the contemporary ethnographic evidence. It is really a rather lazy way to derive a description, which produces, without any real evidence, a prehistoric world that is populated by hunter-gatherers who resemble the modern ones typified by such as the San and the Tlinglit.

We believe that this is not good archaeological practice. Archaeologists accept the uniformitarian principles of geology. This means that natural processes that operated in the past are the same as those that can be observed today, and it forms an essential underpinning to much of our physical evidence – the accumulation of stratigraphic layers and their disruption.

This trans-disciplinary background may explain the initial acceptance of standard present-day social models, but it is harder to explain why it has persisted for so long. An overall development model of band, tribe, chiefdom and state became standard in anthropology, but its continued application to early prehistory and to hunter-gathering in the past is particularly striking. Binford (2001) relies fundamentally on uniformitarian principles in his enormously detailed use of ethnographic data. Unfortunately, all this has meant that archaeology, by simply borrowing models from the present and imposing them on the past, has made little contribution to hunter-gatherer studies in general.

The ethnographic present

This brings us back to our first problem with stereotypes – the assumption that modern hunter-gatherers make good analogues for the past, an assumption that underpins much of what we criticize in this chapter. The equation between past and present was part and parcel of the idea that modern hunter-gatherers, whether they were more primitive and animal-like, or were part of a prelapsarian society, were living representatives of a past way of life. By and large, archaeologists took up this idea uncritically, accepting the social evolutionary models of the Victorian age. In 1911, William Sollas published *Ancient Hunters and their Modern Representatives,* which made explicit comparisons between hunter-gatherers in the modern world and those in the past. His Chapter VI discusses the Middle Palaeolithic, Chapter VII the Australian Aborigines, Chapter VIII the Aurignacian Age, Chapter IX the Bushmen, Chapter XI the Magdalenian Age, and Chapter XII The Eskimo. He writes:

> ... it would appear that the surviving races which represent the vanished Paleolithic hunters have succeeded one another over Europe in the order of their intelligence: each has yielded in turn to a more highly developed and

more highly gifted form of man. From what is now the focus of civilization they have one by one been expelled and driven to the uttermost parts of the earth: the Mousterians survive in the remotely related Australians at the Antipodes, the Solutrians are represented by the Bushmen of the southern extremity of Africa, the Magdalenians by the Eskimo on the frozen margin of the North American continent and as well, perhaps, by the Red Indians. (Sollas 1911: 382-3)

While few of today's writers would be as explicit as this in associating past and present hunter-gatherers, the expectation remains central, that present-day peoples provide us with a frame of reference for understanding past diversity. Such images can certainly still be found in popular accounts, as demonstrated in our preface. But in fact there are many reasons to question how relevant modern hunter-gatherer societies are to an understanding of ancient peoples.

As we said at the beginning of this account, living hunter-gatherers were first really recognized and described when Western colonialism developed. It is therefore hard to separate them from this process, including the need to identify them as primitive, and therefore in need of moral, religious and educational help in order to allow them to progress. Hunter-gatherers have been transformed by contact, which could have resulted in changes to their social organization, such as an increase in their level of mobility as a mechanism for avoiding contact (see below for further discussion of this point). Colonizing powers often did not realize that changes had taken place, and were more concerned with classifying the people as they were encountered. Colonial administrators in some cases may have been responsible for fixing people in economic modes that had no great history. (See also Spriggs 2008 and Roscoe 2009 for a discussion of the significance of history in the use of archaeological analogies for European Neolithic communities.)

There are no cases of modern hunter-gatherer societies that

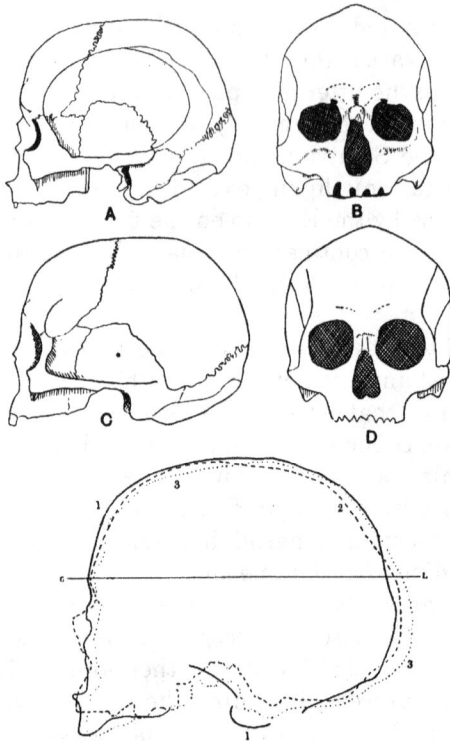

4. These figures were initially presented in William Sollas' *Ancient Hunters and their Modern Representatives* (3rd edn, 1924). The skulls above are 'The Magdalenian skull of Chancelade (A,B) and a recent Eskimo skull (C,D)' (p. 590) and the outlines below compare 'Profiles of (1), the 5. Chancelade skull; (2), the Crô-Magnon skull, and (3) the skull of an Eskimo ...' (p. 591); the Magdalenian and Crô-Magnon skulls are both archaeological examples, from the Upper Palaeolithic of Europe. The text states that: 'The evidence could scarcely be more definitive; the osteological characters of the Eskimo, which are of a very special kind, are repeated by the Chancelade skeleton so completely as to leave no reasonable doubt that it represent the remains of a veritable Eskimo, who lived in southern France during the Magdalenian age' (p. 591).

subsist a hundred per cent on wild resources. The definition of the category in the modern world always has to take this into account. Not only are traded resources available, but most hunter-gatherer societies include individuals who work, or

40

have worked, for other people and who have therefore lived for some time in different economically defined modes. This work may well include direct engagement in farming activities, such as their frequent employment as shepherds. Other forms of relationship exist, such as reliance on welfare payments, which notoriously distort former social patterns. The weakened association between hunter-gatherer societies and subsistence has no doubt been an important influence on recent anthropological models that have moved, either away from subsistence as the defining characteristic (Bird-David 1990), or which have emphasized the overlap with other small-scale societies (for example, Ellen 1982, Lee 1988, Woodburn 1982). Some of the most striking examples of the modernity of hunter-gatherers include pictures of Inuits using rifles and snowmobiles to hunt, while claiming traditional hunting rights – such as the right to hunt whales (see Fig. 5). Such images jar with stereotypes both of hunter-gatherers and of wildlife conservation, but in terms of their relationships to the land and the resources found within it, the Inuit are continuing and adapting the traditions of their ancestors. The fact that they are using modern technology does

5. Bombardier all-terrain vehicle in the Saint-Laurent Metis (Manitoba, Canada) section of the exhibit 'Our Lives', NMAI Mall Museum 9/1/2005, a clear illustration of a traditional society living in the contemporary world.

not change the basic definition of their way of life. It is a vivid demonstration that hunter-gatherer societies are neither 'pure' nor are they contemporary analogues of the past. They are extremely diverse – and modern! There are also no ethnographically recorded hunter-gatherers who do not have contacts with non-hunter-gatherers, whether with Western society, or with other local farming or pastoralist societies.

The archaeological assumption of the 'originality' of simple hunter-gatherers is also stretched to incredulity, when we consider the revisionist debate within the anthropological world, about how long many such societies have been around. In South Africa there has been considerable questioning as to whether many of the San were once farmers (or more accurately, herders – cultivation is rare in the Kalahari), or used to have war chiefs, in a society that would have been very far from the stereotypical form adopted in archaeological analogy. One possible reason for recent historical change is another consequence of living in the modern world. Almost all recent hunter-gatherers have lived, or still live, in parts of the world that are marginal for farming, and some have been forced into these locations relatively recently, changing their lifestyle in the process. The hunter-gatherers of the Pleistocene-Holocene boundary who concern us frequently lived in rich well-watered environments, relatively teeming with resources, whether terrestrial or marine. One does not have to believe that the environment determines all aspects of hunter-gatherer societies to question the basis for analogies between these communities and desert or arctic dwellers.

Present-day boreal hunter-gatherers are considered more appropriate than present-day Aborigines from the Australian desert for comparison with hunter-gatherers of the northern European Holocene. The justification for such linkages is associated with the very strong trend towards ecological analyses of hunting and gathering populations, which are often carried out in precisely the same frameworks as the analysis of animal behaviour. History and agency are ignored while an emphasis on the 'natural' qualities of hunter-gatherers and their relationship with the world helps us to assume that their behaviour is predictable, responding to environmental conditions and changes, and allowing universal analogies to be invoked. Hunter-gatherers are perceived as not fully human, possibly even beyond conversion and education, marginalizing them in a way that would have been recognizable to those who wiped out the Tasmanians, or even to those who conducted the more recent nineteenth- and twentieth-century programmes of fostering Aboriginal children, or the use of residential schools in Canada (Brody 2001).

Discussion

We began this chapter by asking the question: *what is a hunter-gatherer?* Following on from this we ask, *what does it signify to us that so much of human history is that of hunter-gatherering?* We hope to have shown that answers to such seemingly straightforward questions are difficult. The very concept of hunter-gatherers is a particular modern construct, which attempts to describe a notably diverse group of people. There are such people, of course, still living in the modern world, and they have been profoundly influenced by it – so much so that the use of present-day hunter-gatherers as a point of comparison with past ones must be questioned. The economic basis of modern hunter-gatherer societies is seen less and less as their fundamental common feature. In the next chapter we will consider other ways of approaching small-scale societies.

We hope to have shown that problems are incurred by the uncritical use of the concept of hunter-gatherer and by the comparison of ancient hunter-gatherers with modern ones. To see things in these ways is to risk looking at the past in the distorting mirror of the present, and prevents us from understanding the full spectrum of human diversity. Our complaint is not against the careful use of analogy in archaeological interpretations. All archaeological practice is inherently analogical. However, the most dangerous analogies are those that are not recognized as such. We contend that the category of hunter-gatherer is not sufficiently recognized as being problematic in itself, and that its use in analogy can lead to even more problematic conclusions. In the next chapter we will continue with such discussions, looking at specific examples of how on the one hand using such categories, or on the other hand not using them, can lead to different definitions of the modern self. We will also move on to a consideration of the second key category of our analysis – the farmers.

2

Who do you think you are?

Hunter-gatherers occupy a special place in the structure
of modern thought so special, that had they not existed
they would certainly have had to have been invented.

(Ingold 1999: 399)

Labels are very important. Many, or most, archaeological ones
are old and well worn, often borrowed from other disciplines.
We often claim that we use them as shorthand, arguing that
the label is only a label, that it is convenient, and that its flaws
are well-known and recognized. Unfortunately, there is lazi-
ness in this approach, and we often end up meaning what the
label says, because that is the nature of labels and shorthand –
the simple fact that they mean something, even if it is vague or
outmoded or not really what we are talking about, results in
our understanding reverting to what it says on the label. For
example, when we talk about a *farmer*, or a *village*, these words
have both the significance and the 'baggage' that come with
them whether we want it or not. *Hunter-gatherers* is another
such label, separate from the trivial and simplistic statement of
their subsistence economics. In the last chapter we examined
several aspects of it which demonstrate that the concept itself
has a history, and we tried to show in particular that the
present-day societies that are described as hunter-gatherers
are very diverse. Then we tried to show also that the use of
these modern peoples as analogues for past human societies
relies on a further series of implicit assumptions – all too often
made uncritically.

45

Inventing the 'other'

In our account of the development of the term, we have already outlined aspects of the intimate relationship between definitions of hunter-gatherers and the modern world. Here we expand on these themes. As we explained in the last chapter, the very concept of hunter-gatherers arose in a particular social context – colonial expansion and the self-definition of the West in the context of its encounter with different ways of life (see also Said 1978). Ways of understanding the hunter-gatherer were ways of understanding what we – meaning the modern West – *were not*; or, to be more precise, *what we no longer were.* As Pluciennik (2004: 28) puts it: 'Though complex, the category of "hunters" was Other to the ideal of seventeenth and eighteenth century European man – property owning farmers with enclosed lands.'

It need not have been this way. The category of a hunter-gatherer society need not have come into being, and need not have taken this form. In the Soviet Union, for example, anthropology was dominated by Marxist-Leninist theory, and this led to a different categorization of human societies (Schweitzer 2001). The Western category of hunter-gatherer was considered to emphasize the *mode of subsistence* (the way in which food was obtained) rather than what was seen in Marxist-Leninist thought as the more historically significant *mode of production* (the way in which productive activity was organized). Emphasis on the development of class relations in society led to the use of the expression *pervobytnoe obshchestvo* (primordial or primitive society) to describe classless societies. They included many hunter-gatherers, but also classless farmers, and it is clear that many non-egalitarian hunter-gatherers do not sit easily in this category. Schweitzer demonstrates that despite some modifications over time, *pervobytnoe obshchestvo* and hunter-gatherer should not be seen as equivalent concepts. For example, the Soviet description was often restricted to Australian and Tasmanian Aboriginal communities, while Siberian hunter-gatherer communities often did not fall within it.

46

2. Who do you think you are?

Pluciennik has described how Asian conceptions were also different (2004). For example the south Asian idea of 'hillmen' and 'forest dwellers' included hunter-gatherers, but only as a minority among pastoralists and swidden cultivators. They lie outside the Hindu system of the sedentary agricultural people, but are interspersed with that population, as part of it, and fulfil an economic role. They do not fulfil a role as the 'other'.

Closer to home, many readers will be familiar with the representation of hunter-gatherers as being the original green or sustainable communities, living in long-term harmony with their environments, and maintaining an intimate knowledge of their world. This categorization is closely linked to the broader fetishization of indigeneity and authenticity in the modern capitalist system. In the context of our discussion of hunter-gatherers, it is also critically linked to models of hunter-gatherers being *in* nature rather than farmers being *opposed to* nature (see discussion in Ingold 2000), living their lives on a small scale, as opposed to the larger impact of farmers, and at a level of community dynamism perceived as static in terms of historical change, as opposed to the forward-driving farmers. Shepard Krech III (1999) has examined the mobilization in North America of representations of the 'Ecological Indian' since the 1970s, in the context of entwined debates about environment and climate change, indigeneity, authenticity and global capital. If you add to this a smattering of New Age mysticism, you can recognize the powerful twenty-first-century moral and political use of hunter-gatherers as exemplars of green conservationists. Descriptions of this sort are clearly being provided as an alternative to our urban ways of life. Yet to describe *past* hunter-gatherers in these terms is anachronistic. Twenty-first-century notions of a sustainable way of life, or of ecological conservation, would not have been familiar to a nineteenth-century Plains Indian in North America. Krech claims, however, that Native Americans were skilled promoters of their environments, with a detailed understanding of cause and effect relationships, who in many cases would perpetuate the existence of their environments for

47

future generations. But they engaged with that environment through a radically different epistemological framework, including central notions of the reincarnation of prey animals. As Krech puts it:

> The Indians ... were motivated to obtain the necessary resources and desired goods in proper ways. Many believed that animals returned to be killed, sometimes in virtually infinite numbers, as long as hunters demonstrated proper respect. Waste and overkill (as defined by Western conservationists) were apparently largely foreign concepts based in Western science and practice. Indians embraced them as alternatives ways of explaining the decline of deer, beaver and other animals as a result of Western commodification. (Krech 1999: 213)

The relations between hunter-gatherer activity, environmental change and attitudes to the environment are seen here as complex and dynamic. Any notion of hunter-gatherers in the past as 'green' is too simplistic; it appears that once again, hunter-gatherers are being used to represent whatever we are not – small scale, within wild nature, and timeless. Such an account also misses, for example, much evidence of hunter-gatherers over-exploiting wild resources, or of their intervening on a large scale, as with Australian Aboriginal landscape maintenance by scrub burning. Krech also demonstrates that involvement in the fur trade led to significant changes in kill practices by the hunter-gatherers. Once again, the notion that hunter-gatherers might have a political history is eluded by failing to recognize these complex processes of interaction and their outcomes, which may actually spiral unpredictably.

Squatters on the land

Most of our examples in this chapter have drawn on the relationship between near contemporary hunter-gatherers and broader intellectual trends. We now focus on the complex rela-

2. Who do you think you are?

tionship between our narratives about past hunter-gatherers and modern identities. Our initial case-study here is the island of Ireland, and we will examine the ways in which hunter-gatherers figured in Irish archaeological thought in the twentieth century. Foster (2001: 23-32) has stated that the 'self-validation through received memory' of Irish identity operates not only through 'communal acts of remembering and celebration' but also through not talking about certain subjects. Here we propose that by not talking about a hunter-gatherer past, a creation of a specific farming identity was facilitated.

The formation of the Irish state was associated with a strong emphasis on land, soil and stability, themes which had been significant in Irish cultural life even before the nineteenth century. Ferriter (2005: 314) says that in the 1920s and 1930s '... national development was synonymous with agricultural development; [and] that the interests of the farmer and the nation were identical'. This emphasis also contributed to disenfranchisement and discrimination against people who did not conform to these standards, most notably Irish 'Travellers', who were not discriminated against on racial grounds, but on account of their life-style (McLaughlin 1995: 15 & passim: see also McDonagh 1994). Against this background, and given the inevitably and inescapably political role of archaeology in the young state, attitudes to mobile hunter-gatherers in archaeological texts are revealing.

The first chapter of R.A.S. Macalister's *Ancient Ireland: A Study in the Lessons of Archaeology and History* (1935) is entitled 'The fallow land and its earliest inhabitants'. In this title, and in the content of so many other books of this time, the landscape of Ireland simply awaits agriculture. Only at this stage will the Irish story truly begin. The period before agriculture is described as a 'short prologue' (Herity & Eogan 1977: 14-15) an 'episode', or even as *people* 'filling in the time' (Macalister 1949: 13, 22). The hint is clear; that the significant material – the appearance of the Irish peasant – will follow this unfortunate diversion. Against this background, models were constructed that had an impenetrable Irish wild woodland blanketing the country, with Mesolithic activity clinging to the edges. Estyn Evans (1966: 6) wrote of 'fishing on the coasts and hunting at the forest edges'. At one level, this spatial peripheralization of the Mesolithic facilitated the placing of these 'beachcombing' communities at a particular evolutionary stage. At another level, restricting the Mesolithic to the edges of the island served as an important device for 'othering' and marginalizing people who never take ownership of the island, which thus awaits agricultural colonists. Macalister (1935: 8) offers a vivid illustration of these themes:

> ... not for them [the earliest settlers] the vain effort to extract tilth from an unwilling soil, or metal from a stony rock. Not for them a wrestle against principalities and powers. Mere food-gatherers they, parasites upon Nature: content with the molluscs of the shores, with trapped birds or captured fish. Thus easily satisfied, they made no effort to explore the interior of the country, where all was unknown and full of dread ... they shunned the forests, haunted by savage beasts; the noxious swamps, the impassable lakes and rivers. Only by sufferance were they squatters upon a land, which we cannot doubt, their imaginations peopled with demons and hobgoblins. In their time, every strange land was an abode of uncomprehended terrors – the terrors that could be seen, and the yet more terrifying terrors that were invisible.

Mitchell's (1956: 26) description of hunter-gatherers on Sutton Island, just off the Dublin coast, watching the smoke rise from the fires of Neolithic colonists on the mainland, reiterates the same spatialized historical structure. It is also important to note that Macalister clearly argues from a modern cultural perspective, interestingly foreshadowing the idea of a fear of the wild that informs Hodder's (1990) perspectives on the difference between farming and pre-farming societies and the complex suite of attitudes towards woodland that people from farming communities often seem to hold; exemplified for many by the wild woods of Tolkein's Middle Earth or the *Wind in the Willows* (see discussion in Peterken 1996).

An examination of Irish archaeological textbooks as they developed throughout the twentieth century shows that they had consistent themes for pre-farming societies. People's lives are dominated by subsistence, with little or no complexity of social organization. It is a world without sociality, of independent bands clinging on to existence, ignorant of communities beyond the next hill and 'having little or no mutual relationships' (Macalister 1949: 41). Social relations are denied in these accounts; they are replaced by economic ones. This is exacerbated by the traditional emphasis on the arrival of immigrant farming communities at the start of the Neolithic. Macalister again (1928: 41):

> Food gatherers are inevitably squeezed out after the arts of food producing have by any means been established in the regions where they pass their unenterprising existence. Thereafter they cannot compete with their more progressive neighbours in the battle for life; sooner or later they must emigrate or perish.

The hunter-gatherers of Ireland played little or no role in wider historical processes; they were stuck in an eternal seasonal round of coastal exploitation. History was something that happened elsewhere, and began with the arrival of outsiders. Strikingly, this model of society and history is identical to some attitudes to communities of travelling people.

> to the extent that Irish Travellers were perceived as having any history, theirs was not a history in any cumulative or purposeful sense. It is instead an endless cycle of hardship and poverty ... not so much a history as a mythology. They evolved outside the framework of Irish historical time and were confined to 'that which is changeless and eternal' (MacLaughlin 1995: 37, 38).

6. Much of the evidence for early settlement in northwestern Europe is low key, like these flint flakes and cores from Wicklow Town, Ireland.

Given the central role of sedentism and farming to Irish identity, the strong parallels between the attitudes expressed towards two mobile communities – and two alternative ways of life – are not surprising.

These emphases are not found only in books from the early twentieth century. In almost all introductory Irish archaeological texts, the Mesolithic period receives very little discussion, a problem exacerbated by the frequent inclusion of discussions of environmental change in the Mesolithic chapters, a tedious emphasis on subsistence, and the lack of detail on social organization. Even John Waddell's *Prehistoric Archaeology of Ireland* (1998), the most recent textbook on Irish prehistory, continues many of these trends. Only seventeen of its 378 pages discuss the Mesolithic (4,000 years of Ireland's prehistory) and four of these are given over to a discussion of the changing environments of the Holocene era, which makes no reference to archaeology: thirteen pages then summarize the Mesolithic. In contrast, in the account of the late Bronze Age (900-600 BC), weapons alone are given seven pages. Differences in the nature of the data available are, of course, important in determining the extent of the discussion of the periods, but it is hard to escape the impression that the construction of these narratives marginalizes the hunter-gatherers of Ireland, who are still being presented as of little or no significance, and whose lives are dominated by subsistence economics. As in our wider picture, those who are not settled farmers, ancient or modern, are incapable of change and make no impact. The history of Ireland, it appears, begins with the Neolithic.

Farming stereotypes: the wild and the tame

These attitudes to the difference between hunter-gatherers and farmers belong to the mainstream. Despite most of us having an urban background, and most of our experience of the rural world being of very modern industrial farming or carefully maintained 'wilderness', the archaeological literature often assumes that we have something in common with farmers. When we discuss hunter-gatherers we are talking about an 'other' and our terminology tends to reflect this. Hunter-gatherer sites are described as 'flint scatters', or 'base camps'. Societies are egalitarian, cosmology is described as shamanistic or magical. Farmers live in hamlets and villages, they have religion, and they think like us. The images conjured up are a mixture of a William Morris ideal of farmers in smocks with straw between their teeth, French catholic peasants trooping to confession, and a vision of timeless *fellahin* in Oriental villages who form a backdrop to the West's Orientalist encounter with the Middle East. This sounds like a caricature, but it is a caricature created by some fairly influential archaeologists, and also by the images that are used to portray their finds. Illustrations in popular archaeology books may show hunter-gatherers as hairy men with bows and arrows, shooting dangerous animals in wild surroundings overshadowed by dark, lightning-streaked skies, while early farmers are shown with the women nursing babies, in thoroughly domesticated, regularly ploughed, tidy landscapes, beneath benign skies. Some reconstruction drawings would seem to suggest that trousers (for men only, of course) and razors were part of the Neolithic revolution. Returning to our theme of farming stereotypes, Jacques Cauvin (2000), a highly respected French archaeologist and one of the most influential thinkers of his generation in Neolithic studies, stressed the emergence of peasants, and the birth of the gods. According to him, we are supposed to share a fear of the terrible earth mother and to be able to comprehend and share the rich symbolic imagery of the early Neolithic, in a way we cannot do with its hunter-gatherer antecedents. Cauvin sums up the entire Palaeolithic as an 'enormous period of latency ... that separate[s] the emergence of man from his taking charge of his environment, which [is what] appears normal today' (p. 1). Until then, we were 'just like any other predatory species'. Along with its emphases, again, on historical agency and on being inside or outside of nature, this is clearly a story about *them* and *us*. In the English-speaking world, Ian Hodder (1990) separated the world into wild and tame. Again, we are assumed to identify with this division, and to sit firmly on the domestic side of the fence.

The division that puts us with farmers as safe and familiar, part of our world, as opposed to the marginal and dangerous hunter-gatherers, is an aspect of the series of dichotomies into which we categorize our world. As indicated at the beginning of this section, we also divide the modern world into rural and urban, farming into industrial and traditional, landscapes as farmed or wilderness. Some of the divisions have been extensively debated. Said's discussion (1978) of Orientalism revealed how such concepts as the traditional Oriental village were used to create the idea of a passive East as opposed to the dynamic modern West. Ironically, when archaeologists deploy the Oriental village into the Neolithic they carry the anachronisms into the past, not least in images of the recent landscape with its villages, herds of sheep and camels (e.g. the cover of *Village on the Euphrates* by Moore, Hillman & Legge 2000). There is a frequent discussion of modern 'traditional' village architecture in comparison with the prehistoric (Kinzel 2006). Foster McCarter (2007: 85) states that 'in many places village architecture has not changed since the Neolithic'. The very description of the new, increasingly sedentary communities as 'villages' carries a great weight of associated ideas with it. The use of 'hamlet' to describe small settlements, especially in the Natufian, brings in a word, that is normally little used outside a romanticized countryside, to evoke bucolic tranquillity in what was clearly a pre-agricultural and still substantially mobile society.

These notions of timeless Oriental villages provide a link to a provocative recent discussion by Clive Gamble (2007) which suggests that Childe's discussion of the Neolithic revolution in Asia was a narrative designed to effect certain political ends, particularly to counter totalitarianism. Childe, said Gamble, essentially used the Orient as a historical theatre. This provided a time and place for agricultural origins, but it was the later development from these origins that was of interest to Childe, especially in terms of self-government and state formation. Thus, western Europe can be seen to develop from the Asian origins of agriculture and, in Childe's trajectory, transcend these Oriental origins: 'the Neolithic revolution becomes the origin point of the modern project of European history and culture that gained definition by opposing and containing the Orient' (Gamble 2007: 31). The Orient, in a classically Orientalist discussion, is frozen, passive, and feminine, in the face of male European historical dynamism.

The diversity of farming societies

The transition from hunter-gatherer to farmer requires us to have people we define as 'other' on one side of the divide and people we describe as 'like us' on the other. This also means that however long we see the process as taking, it remains a major step change with a clear beginning and an end. The opposition between them makes it hard to introduce the idea of transition. We hope we have demonstrated that this step-change mentality relies on stereotypes, and we have spent some time exploring the ways in which the hunter-gatherer operates as the 'other'. But farming and farmers are also complex, varied and diverse, and this category also requires critical attention.

One way by which we can try to escape from our farming stereotypes is to consider the diversity of practices that are generally summed up as 'farming'. They range from the giant modern industrial processes that we are most familiar with (even though we claim an empathy with an uncertainly dated but somehow more traditional form of farming, which may have vanished in the UK with the eighteenth- and nineteenth-century enclosure acts!), to the small-scale garden-plot type of farming known in anthropology as 'horticulture' (although the term is used much more broadly outside anthropology), typically characterized by small plots and mixed crops, which we might know from allotments or cottage gardens. Perceived in this way, the economic practices of farming suddenly appear much less demanding than our conventional image of farm labour (could hunter-gatherers farm at the weekend just as modern urban gardeners do?). We can see that in fact it is possibly less seasonally demanding than the hunter-gathering that relies on salmon runs, or on the sudden appearance of migratory animals. Other forms of farming exist today, including slash-and-burn, or swidden, which is still used in some places, typically where the soil becomes easily exhausted and plots have to be moved. Swidden farmers generally have very high rates of mobility, sometimes higher than those of many hunter-gatherers, as reflected in the alternative term 'shifting agriculture'.

One of the recognized problems facing any discussion of early farming is that there are difficulties in the definition of agriculture and associated terms (see, for example, Harris 1989, 1996, 2007). In 2007 (p. 18) he writes that 'agriculture and domestication are prime examples of imprecise catch-all concepts that create confusion because users of them tend to assume that others share the same, usually intuitive and seldom explicitly stated, understanding of what they mean'. He notes the use of prefixes and adjectives to qualify the terms agriculture and domestication, such as 'proto-', 'incipient', 'intensive', 'behavioural', and 'cultural', to name but a few, but observes that the meanings of these are rarely made clear. The use of a wide range of other terms, such as 'food production', 'gardening', and 'horticulture', appears impressive, but is ultimately only confusing. According to Vrydaghs and Denham (2007: 2) these problems are most acute for precisely the topic that interests us most, 'differentiating early agriculture from other practices'. These authors provide a summary of many of the problems and of efforts to overcome them, such as attempts to develop a new terminology for intermediate categories, calls to abandon the use of the term altogether, the distinction between definitions based on social dependence on domesticated species or on the genetic and morphological definition of such species. They sum up by stating (p. 5) that

... lack of a clear definition for agriculture, particularly early agriculture, reflects its multifaceted nature. The resultant porosity of the concept of agriculture mirrors a diffuseness in its geographical, social and temporal manifestations in the past. From such a perspective, there is less of a concern with identifying cores/peripheries and centres/non-centres; rather we begin to see a diffuseness manifest as asynchronies and mosaics of practice related to cultivation, domestication and environmental transformation in diverse social contexts.

Although they are seeing these things very much from a non-Eurasian perspective, it is clear that many of their ideas are relevant to our debate. The move away from ideas of core areas has begun to be taken up in southwest Asia, with concepts of polycentrism or mosaics of interaction becoming more prevalent (Warburton 2004, Rollefson and Gebel 2004, Gebel 2004). The concept of diffuseness is also very useful in attempting to break down rather fixed ideas of what agriculture might be, and in emphasizing the importance of local differences, rather than accepting the smoothed picture provided for regional syntheses. Porosity is also a helpful concept, as it covers the ambiguities of definition both for transitional periods, and for societies that do incorporate significant aspects of both foraging and agricultural economies – such as those identified by Bird-David (1999) in south Asia – and indeed for societies in which agriculture appears to be a 'take it or leave it' option.

We know that there are ancient practices that lie outside our varied modern images of farming and gardening. In southwest Asia, it is clear that for a long time people were cultivating wild plants. The range of human input presumably includes all sorts of possibilities, from the collecting and sowing of seeds and roots, weeding, watering, and going on to guarding. Most conceptions of farming, horticulture and gardening include at their heart a measure of caring for the soil. One of the things we do not know is when and how soil management emerged within the range of practices involved in early farming. There may be glimpses in the southern Levant where, in the early Neolithic, settlements appear to contain their rubbish in structured midden dumps, to the later Neolithic where a halo of material surrounds the site, which may suggest they were spreading their waste to manure the soil (Kuijt, Finlayson & MacKay 2007). Bogaard argues that in the early Neolithic of southeast and central Europe 'growing conditions of high soil disturbance and productivity were maintained artificially, with high inputs of labour (e.g. manuring/middening, tillage and weeding)' (2005, 183). Soil maintenance would seem to be so fundamental to modern farming and gardening that it is difficult to really discuss farming until it emerges. Unfortunately, many strategies, such as crop rotation and the practice of leaving some fields fallow, are hard to detect archaeologically. We do not know what activities became routine practices, or for how long. It is important that we should not see them as stepwise evolutionary changes towards farming, but as chronologically and spatially distinct practices.

2. Who do you think you are?

There remains a widely accepted idea that agriculture requires plants to have become morphologically domesticated (Harris 1989, Ford 1985) and that the tending of wild plants was a pre-agricultural practice. While Ford thought that these things were parts of a series of evolutionary stages, neither Harris nor Rindos (1984) saw them as unidirectional, nor indeed as separate stages, but as parts of continuous processes. More recently, Harris has given increased attention to what he describes as the ' "in-between" systems of animal protection and plant management that are neither foraging nor farming' (Harris 2007: 20), a category which he believes has existed in many parts of the world, but which is hard to identify in the past and has therefore been largely ignored by archaeologists, who have focused on societies that are clearly either hunter-gatherer or agricultural. We suspect that while this in-between category may have been looked at in some ethnoarchaeological approaches, the scarcity of identifications may also be related to the archaeological urge to define societies as one thing or the other.

Cultivation covers a wide range of practices, many of them employed by people classified as hunter-gatherers – many of whom, however, are clearly not on some development path leading to agriculture. The tending of wild plants, including activities such as land clearance, vegetation burning, planting and weeding, might better be described as non-agricultural cultivation. A similar set of activities involving the management of wild animals has an equivalent status. Smith (2001) describes all such systems as 'low-level food production', which he sees as distinct both from hunting and gathering and from farming. While the term appears useful, the creation of another distinct category seems less so, just when we are increasingly recognizing the diffuseness and porosity of small-scale or early agricultural societies.

In northwest Europe considerable amounts of evidence suggests complex relationships linking 'wild' and 'domestic' animals with human populations – of both hunter-gatherers and farmers. Extensive discussion has focused on hunter-gatherer

59

management of plant resources, including the deliberate burning of vegetation so as to promote plant growth, in order to encourage wild animals to congregate in open spaces (e.g. Mellars 1976). An increasing amount of work in Britain and Ireland as well as in south Scandinavia (Zvelebil 2008) suggests that hunter-gatherers actively introduced non-domesticated animals, including boar and deer, to island environments, suggesting complex strategies of management of animals and landscapes. At La Grande-Rivoire, Isère, in France, a brown bear mandible shows growth deformities that suggest that the animal had been forced to wear a bit or halter from when it was four to seven months old until its death at the age of five or six years (Chaix, Bridault & Picavet 1997). In southern Scandinavia 'domesticated' dogs were given formal burials with grave goods, and at the cemetery of Skateholm a dog's burial included more grave goods than any other burial (Larsson 1990). Simple notions of 'wild' and 'domestic', 'human' and 'animal' do not appear relevant here. Lewis-Williams and Pearce (2005: 141) believe that in southwest Asia conceptual 'domestication' of aurochs (wild cattle) in the context of ritual and ceremonial practice predated the origins of herding. Even in the Neolithic, red deer, a 'wild animal', appear to have been introduced to the island of Ireland by farmers (Woodman, McCarthy & Monaghan 1997). In Late Neolithic Orkney red deer were actively managed in the context of the agricultural settlement of the Orkney islands. At times they were slaughtered in large numbers, often at the edges of settlements, and near boundary walls, seemingly being kept separate from other resources: Sharples argues that the red deer was conceptually ambiguous, 'placed between the wild and the domestic' and held a special significance unrelated to their economic worth (Sharples 2000: 113-14). Such evidence suggests that categorical distinctions between 'wild' and 'domestic' animals in either farming or hunter-gatherer contexts should be treated with caution.

People perceive their world in different ways, but they are often divided by archaeologists and anthropologists by a hard line separating hunter-gatherers from farmers. The fuzzy boundary between, at one extreme, assisting wild plants to grow and, at the other, controlled farming of domestic varieties, would suggest that no such hard line is likely to exist. It has been said that, while no modern hunter-gatherers subsist entirely on wild resources, the percentage of non-wild resources is always small, normally less than 5%, and that there is a clear gap between them and societies who rely on cultivated resources for more than 45% of their consumption (Panter-Brick, Layton & Rowley-Conwy 2001: 3). Such statistics do not attempt to distinguish between the cultivation of wild or domestic resources, and this lack of distinction remains a significant problem in prehistory, Nevertheless, in spite of this omission and their rather mechanistic nature, the statistics have been used to insist that there *is* a division.

One feature of many farming practices is that there are often connections that are simply built into the activities by their very nature. Animals may be needed for manure or for traction, particular plants may be needed for crop rotation as well as simply for consumption, and so on; indeed it is the 'package' created by the combination of domestic animals and domestic crops that is frequently seen as the basis for the rapid expansion of agriculture from southwest Asia (e.g. Bogaard 2005). These connections may deepen the gap between modern hunter-gatherers who rely mostly on wild resources, and other modern small-scale societies, which may rely on more than 45% domestic resources, not because of any binary opposition, but simply as a result of the complementary activities. They may also permit a distinction to be made between perceptions of simply helping nature, to perceptions of tending the soil. In farming societies, activities such as hunting are not seen to dilute their essentially farming character, and may be interpreted as being practised for prestige or ritual ends, rather than as part of the real economy. Such discussions, of course, beg discussion of what 'hunting' might mean in the context of animals such as the red deer on Neolithic Orkney, outlined above, while southwest Asian Pre-Pottery Neolithic societies seem to have existed within what is now the gap between contemporary hunter-gatherers and other small-scale societies.

The practices both of hunting and gathering and of farming are deeply contextualized – the decisions about how to divide up the tasks and the produce, and of what to grow and how, are not taken from a clean slate. To return to the Marxist-Leninist language with which we began this chapter, there is a difference between the mode of subsistence and the mode of production. The anthropology of development, examining why and when people adopt new technologies and practices, shows very clearly that even where overseas development agencies can demonstrate clear economic gain, the take-up will be poor, unless the innovations can be presented in a way that is congruent with current practice. We can readily accommodate such insights within our understanding of the operative agencies. One of the problems with discussions of the transition to the Neolithic is that the debate rapidly ceases to be concerned with what people are doing on a human scale, and becomes focused on grand models that explain everything, or on the biological processes that produce domesticated plants and animals. Processes like these are important, but they have to operate within human societies, and within this limitation we have to consider the role of the various agencies that are at work, and the varied nature of individual communities on a local or regional scale.

If we can accept that prehistoric hunter-gatherers and farmers were diverse in their practices, then it becomes easier to reach the point where we realize that trying to categorize any society as either one or the other may not be important. This is perhaps the starting point for interest in 'small-scale societies' (Ellen 1982), which specifically puts horticulturalists together with foragers. Woodburn (1982) also broke down the barrier between modes of subsistence by using the term 'egalitarian societies', and these two authors were followed by Lee (1988), with his idea of a 'communal mode of production'. More recent anthropological trends have begun to link small-scale societies with marginal groups, including first-world urban groups such as beggars and gypsies (Guenther 2007). Kelly (1995), in *The*

2. Who do you think you are?

Foraging Spectrum, discusses the nature of seasonal foragers (for example the Mikea from Madagascar), who rely on wild resources in some seasons but may become horticulturists or do any kind of paid work at other times. He stresses the historical context of hunting and gathering, and the common reliance of foragers on government aid, wage labour, trade, or even 'commercial foraging' (Kelly 1995: 25), as well as the retreat into increasingly marginal environments. The notion of there being any hard and fast boundary in such a situation is difficult to sustain. Fowler and Turner (1999: 420) refer to a 'continuum of activities relating to the intensification of food supplies', which may be seen as simply emphasizing the gradual nature of change. Even more interestingly, they note (p. 421) that 'Hunter-gatherers are seen as domesticating their environment even though they may not have domesticated individual species of plants or animals'. This is a strikingly fundamental idea. Hunter-gatherers do not inhabit their landscape in and of nature, as animals do. They use many methods to maintain and enhance their environment, including both practical ones such as burning of scrub, and those that are found in many of their religious and ceremonial activities. To understand the world in their terms, when animals are recognized as kin or as spirits, it brings them into a human world as much as it brings people into a natural one. Hodder's well known separation of wild and domestic implies a very modern, Western perspective on how to divide the world, as do any attempts to describe non-farming societies as pre-human or non-human. Anthropologists such as Descola (2005) have done much to illustrate how both foragers and horticulturists have a far more complex attitude towards the surrounding world than any dichotomous stance would allow.

Discussion

In this chapter we hope to have demonstrated that the use of the label 'hunter-gatherer' can be seen to carry significant political baggage and serve particular political purposes. We might *hope* that archaeologists would be sensitive to all of the nuances involved, but in reality this seems unlikely, given some of the forms of representation employed. In many instances, the political effects sought by use of these labels are deliberate, and unavoidable. Alongside this labelling, the pervasive influence of dichotomous analysis, whose subjects must be either farmers or hunter-gatherers, can be seen to restrict our understanding of diversity, past and present. Thinking critically about the wild and the tame, and about the nature of relationships between people and the world around them, especially in terms of subsistence, also highlights the diversity of past and present activity and the difficulty in using simple labels to classify the people involved.

3

Farming and the origins of villages

Abu Hureyra is one of the few archaeological sites in the world to have revealed the remains of a settlement of hunters and gatherers that developed into a village of early farmers. (Moore, Hillman & Legge 2000: v)

Farming is an integral part of the modern world, and modern industrial farming is essential to sustaining our way of life. In archaeology, farming is seen as the key shift that freed people from dependence on the natural world, raised the ceiling on food production, allowed the production of surpluses, and set us on the road to modernity. In particular, the adoption of agriculture is often associated with storage, sedentism, social change, specialization, the development of urban life, and ultimately 'civilization'. The significance of farming cannot be overstated, but perhaps some of its ramifications can. Farming may be a vital component in the development of urbanism, but does not automatically produce it. Statements of what is required for urbanism have been debated at length in Bronze Age archaeology of the Near East. We will not go over them in any detail here, but one important point to note is that urbanism is not simply related to a concentration of the population, but also has other social, economic and political attributes. In particular, we need to be extremely cautious, as ever, in ascribing subsequent developments to earlier changes. The archaeology of origins seeks for the earliest manifestations of phenomena, and the complex pattern of developments that farming makes possible are no exception.

In many narratives the initial shift from mobile to sedentary life-styles is conflated with the pervasive and powerful political model of the village. Here it is important to be precise: the term village in a narrow sense simply refers to a small group of houses (normally, but not invariably, permanent). But the term also carries strong political and emotive resonance in the context of models of rural settlement, and, critically for our argument, may allow for some slippage between a description of a small settlement and an expectation of a particular form of social organization; notably through associations with peasantry. Thus the village can be presented as a familiar feature of the past: Susan Foster McCarter (2007), for example, offers an image of a village with the caption: 'As can be seen in this Anatolian village with its communal threshing ground, the principles of village organization invented in the Neolithic are still followed today' (her Figure 9.3), where such 'principles' ultimately mean little more than a distinction between private space and public space. Making such links is all about origins – the origins and development of traditional peasant villages in the Near East and in Europe, and how aspects of the modern West have transcended this trajectory. A classically Orientalist structure.

Yet the evidence suggests something rather different from any kind of 'village' that would be familiar to us, even where it suggests increasingly sedentary behaviour in gradually bigger communities, as it does in southwest Asia. Here, in the Pre-Pottery Neolithic B (PPNB, 10,500-8,700 calibrated years BP), the large settlements known as megasites are best understood not as 'villages' but as something for which we have no ready analogue, completely different from anything produced by our present-day life-styles. These societies form our first case-study in this chapter. Our second case-study shows how the notion of an association between agricultural production and tightly clustered settlement may be broken down by a consideration of non-nucleated agricultural communities. Such an observation is not original, but our case-study, western Ireland, highlights how a fierce modern debate between the proponents of different models of how a community should be spatially organized, as either nucleated or non-nucleated. These Irish examples suggest that the relationship between agriculture and villages is deeply problematic, and that the debates reflect our contemporary world. Our third study is concerned with the stereotypes that have been used to describe the original rural settled landscape in discussions of the Natufian.

We should also note that farming does not correlate with sedentism on a one-to-one basis. Living in one place relies on an abundance of resources and either their availability over many seasons of the year or the ability to store them. Farming is only one way of making this possible. American northwest coast communities provide the classic example of complex hunter-gatherer societies, living in villages without farming, but with many of the social patterns more normally associated with farmers. On the other hand, many forms of farming, as noted elsewhere, require greater mobility than is found among some of the hunter-gatherers. However, in archaeological thought, sedentism and farming remain closely associated, and general statements can be found quite commonly, such as: 'Archaeologists are particularly interested in why humans, after such a long period of time as gatherers and hunters, settled down and then began to farm and herd animals' (Byrd 2005: 231).

Megasites and the imagination

The development of urban societies is a good example of the interplay between our preconceptions and our search for origin points for the development of agriculture and the origins of villages. The association between farming and villages appears as so fundamental that at times the start of the Neolithic in southwest Asia has even been described as the beginning of 'village culture'. Byrd (2005: 232) wrote recently that 'Larger food-producing villages then emerged abruptly during the Early Neolithic as a socially driven, opportunistic strategy that artificially created, through cultivation, an expandable resource and surplus', making very clear his association between villages and food production or farming. So central is this question that Cauvin 2000, Özdogan 1997 and Watkins 1997 have debated whether the term Neolithic should be associated with the appearance of villages, rather than with the appearance of agriculture.

In the southern Levant the pattern of increasing sedentism from the Early Natufian on into the Neolithic is well known, and in synthetic accounts is usually presented as a given. We discuss later some of the problems with this straightforward evolutionary model, but in this case-study we will focus on the emergence of larger settlements, the so-called 'megasites' in the PPNB of the southern Levant. Here there was an apparently gradual increase in scale and degree of sedentism from the Pre-Pottery Neolithic A (PPNA, 12,000-10,500 calibrated years BP) into the Early PPNB (10,500-10,100 calibrated years BP) and Middle PPNB (10,100-9,250 calibrated years BP), Then, in the Late PPNB (9,250-8,700 calibrated years BP) large settlements appear, up to 14 hectares in size, such as 'Ain Ghazal, Basta, Wadi Shweib and others (see Fig. 7). They are characterized by densely packed rectilinear architecture, often with good evidence for two storeys, and with a new attention to planning in the separation of residential and non-residential buildings. Although precise population estimates can always be debated, it is clear that both the numbers of people present and the density of settlement increased markedly, to produce populations measured in their thousands. 'Megasite' is in some ways a good term, in that it is neutral regarding the nature of these settlements. However, despite this neutrality, there is an underlying assumption that these megasites are a reflection of an overall evolutionary path to increasingly large sites, connecting the megasites to the substantially later process of urbanism that occurs in the Bronze Age in this region. However, urbanism is not only about the size of a community, but also about organization, and particularly the emergence of specialist skilled workers and elites. Gary Rollefson (1997) has concluded that the LPPNB is marked by a significant change in the way society is organized, and various scholars, for example

7. The Late PPNB site of Basta, Jordan, is located by a spring on the edge of the semi-arid steppe, still used by the modern village. The buildings are densely spaced and the architecture is sophisticated and well-made. Comparisons are often made with the traditional farming village: one immediate difference that can be seen here is between the tightly clustered prehistoric village and the widely scattered nineteenth-century layout.

Quintero and Wilke (1995), have pointed to the presence of specialists, especially the highly skilled flint knappers who produced the so-called bipolar naviform cores and blades. Both the level of skill required and the apparent presence of specialized working areas have been used to infer that dedicated specialists were at work. In further support of the view that social complexity was developing at these large sites, there have been explanations put forward to account for specialized ritual buildings, variously labelled as shrines or temples (Rollefson 1998). The activities conducted at these settlements have been variously seen as the foundations of the earliest real religious behaviour, and as further evidence for the growing presence of elites and specialists and a connection between 'religion' and early villages is often made (see Chapter 5 below). Some scholars have taken these lines of evidence as indications of early or 'proto-' urbanism.

There are, however, various fundamental problems with accounts that see these settlements as evidence for some form of early urbanism, or as lying on a direct evolutionary path to it. The most obvious difficulty is that around the end of the PPNB the megasites collapse (some decline earlier, and some continue to be partly occupied, but none really continues in the same way after the PPNB). These large communities are therefore not on a straightforward developmental path to urbanism. The world of the Final PPNB (also called the PPNC, 8,600-8,250 calibrated years BP) appears as a rather different one. Dependence on domestic animals (now including cattle and pigs) becomes almost complete, which appears to indicate a real farming economy, but at the same time the importance of large and elaborate settlements seems to decline. Instead, the world of the subsequent Pottery Neolithic is more dominated by smaller settlements, perhaps best described by the work of Banning (2001) in the Wadi Ziqlab. Recent computer modelling by Barton (Barton *et al.* 2010) has supported suggestions made by Köhler-Rollefson and Rollefson (e.g. 1990) that LPPNB megasite populations seriously damaged their local environment, and this modelling also suggests that the more distributed Pottery Neolithic settlement pattern would have been less damaging. Recent work at Dhra' suggests that Pottery Neolithic populations were also working to protect their environment by terrace building and manuring, indicating a new relationship with the land. There are some substantial

3. Farming and the origins of villages

aceramic Neolithic sites, Çatalhöyük in Anatolia being the most famous, that do continue into the Pottery Neolithic, but their relative scarcity to some extent suggests that they had a more unusual role in the wider landscape, or were preserving some anachronistic trends, rather than representing a main stream of development. Newly settled substantial sites; such as Sha'ar HaGolan (Garfinkel 2004) in the southern Levant and the Tell Sabi Abiad in northern Syria, reveal a new tradition of Neolithic settlement and may indicate a more hierarchical settlement pattern based on the small farming sites. However, even at these new large sites the lack of communal buildings has suggested to some that this is not the case, and that what may be appear to be a single large site is more an agglomeration of houses spread over the landscape and built and used over several hundreds of years (Akkermans et al. 2006).

This issue of settlement density does concern the actual size of the megasites, in particular how much of the site was occupied at any given time. It is difficult to calculate realistic estimates of density for the sites, but it seems likely that they were not always densely occupied. At 'Ain Ghazal, the first megasite to be identified, Rollefson (2001) has noted that the full extent and most dense occupation of the site does not occur until the Late PPNB, when there appears to be a sudden expansion of the population, and he has argued that such a rapid expansion requires the arrival of people from outside. This would raise the question of why people concentrated within these sites at all. For early farming societies the subsequent more scattered settlement pattern of the Pottery Neolithic seems much more sensible, with people living close to their fields. There has been much debate about how the residents of a megasite managed when, presumably, the distance to their crops increased. The combined effect of there being no apparent use of fertilization or soil maintenance, along with the need to fetch wood for fuel and building, must have meant that people had to walk further and further for their daily needs (e.g. Bogaard & Isaakidou 2010). At the most basic level, the large central settlements must have made life harder and

71

harder for their populations, and quite probably eventually caused local ecological disasters. This appears to be the opposite of the Pottery Neolithic landscape, inhabited by people who lived adjacent to their fields and maintained their soil by manuring and terracing. Real urbanism appears to have grown from these later roots, as the smaller agricultural units began to support a hierarchical settlement system.

It would appear therefore that the megasites do not really represent a new urban or even farming society. Even at the level of the basic economy, there is still extensive reliance on the hunting of wild animals during most of the PPNB, and it is only in the course of the LPPNB and into the PPNC that this changes, with domesticated sheep and goat rising to about 70% of bone assemblages, and the full range of domesticated animals, including cattle and pigs, becoming available. Even then, the available resources probably do not include several of the key items found in the developing economies of later periods, such as olives. Some authors (for example, Kuijt 2000a) have thought that for a long time PPNB society was clearly trying to maintain an egalitarian form and resisting the hierarchical tendencies inherent in larger settlements, by maintaining burial practices that do not contain grave goods, by complicated patterns of secondary burials, and by the use of standard architectural forms. In fact we have no need to see this as a deliberate attempt to maintain hunter-gatherer egalitarianism – after all, there are plenty of traditional farming societies that are egalitarian. At least, however, it is very clearly *not* the early development of a hierarchical, proto-urban society nor of what we might immediately recognize as the principles of organization of a village. We can also consider the ceremonial or ritual buildings in this light. Ceremonial buildings at least as sophisticated as those found in PPNB megasites have been built by much smaller communities, from rare examples in the Natufian (e.g. a large building with a plaster bench at 'Ain Mallaha, presumed to have a ritual role), on to increasing numbers of ritual and corporate buildings in the PPNA, especially from the northern Levant at Gobekli Tepe,

Jerf el-Ahmar, and Nemrik. Ceremonial buildings remain a fascinating indication of how the sedentary communities of southwest Asia became an increasingly materialized society, but they are not uniquely a feature of megasites.

Non-nucleated settlements and house societies

The Céide Fields are one of Ireland's most iconic archaeological landscapes (see Figs 8 and 9). Preserved beneath the blanket bogs of North Mayo, and painstakingly surveyed over the years by Seamas Caulfield and generations of students from University College Dublin, the archaeological remains include large-scale regular field systems, more irregular fields, small enclosures, tombs and other features. While it is very difficult to provide a date for the construction of the field systems, a series of dates from pine trees growing in bogs above and near the walls (which lie on mineral soil) suggests that the walls must be Neolithic, while palynological evidence suggests that the main phases of agriculture in the region are Middle Neolithic, *c.* 5600-5200 calibrated years BP. The field systems are likely to be of this date. Early Neolithic houses (c. 5800-5600 calibrated years BP) are known in the region, but the nature of their associated settlement landscape is not clearly understood. It is possible that the regular field systems have their origin in this period. Caulfield's work at Céide Fields and other sites on the North Mayo coast provides a rare opportunity to study a Neolithic settlement landscape rather than small fragments of one. His interpretation of the systems is that they indicate a pastorally based economy with a scattered settlement pattern. The individual enclosures within the regular fields were the locations of settlements (Caulfield 1978, 1983, Caulfield, O'Donnell & Mitchell 1998).

Caulfield grew up and continues to live in North Mayo, and he is passionately devoted to the area and to dealing with some of the challenges it faces in present-day Ireland. In particular, the modern communities of the area have traditionally lived in non-nucleated settlements (see Fig. 10). To take the example of

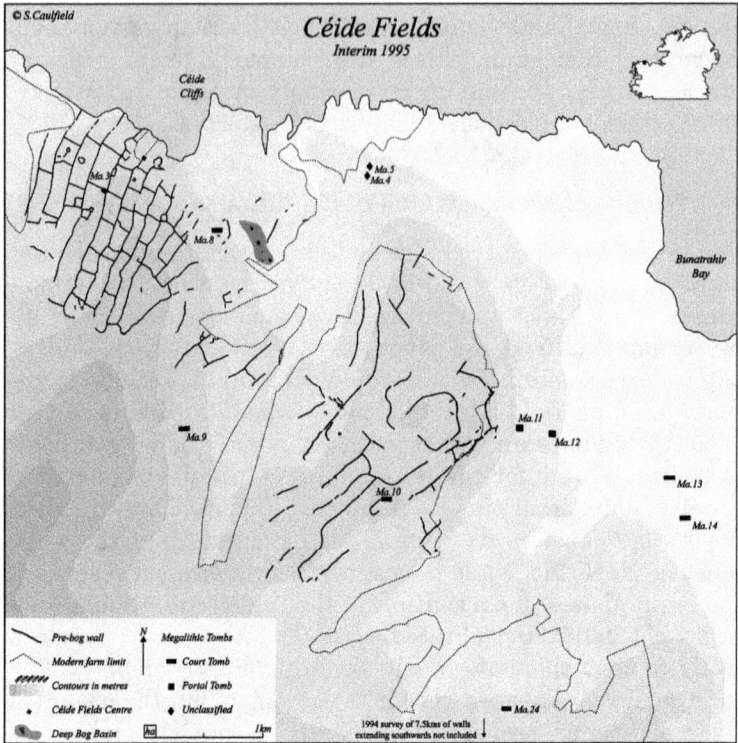

8. The Céide Fields, a Neolithic agricultural landscape preserved beneath blanket bog in North Co. Mayo, Ireland.

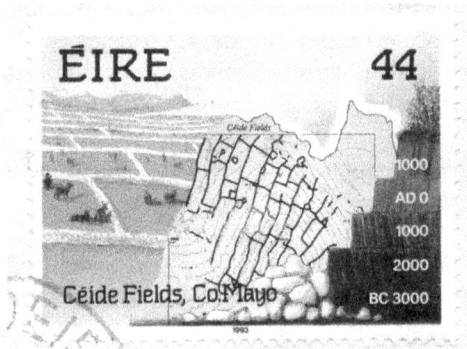

9. The Céide Fields celebrated in a stamp, date of issue 2 September 1993.

10. View of dispersed settlement at Belderrig, North Co. Mayo, Ireland.

Belderrig, Caulfield's home, the 'village' extends across the whole valley but, apart from a clustering of the pub, post office and church, there is no sense of a particular nuclear focus. This model of settlement is perceived as being under threat in Ireland from a paradigm emphasizing nucleated settlement – the assumption that a village should have a centre. We do not need to pass judgment on this debate here, but Caulfield's reconstruction of the Neolithic landscapes certainly did not start from the standpoint of expecting nucleated agricultural villages, and the model he created for the Neolithic is, in the end, reminiscent of the traditional settlement system within which he grew up. This sense of continuity and long-term association is hugely important in the presentation of the archaeology of this region. In Ireland, as in southwest Asia, the contemporary settlement system seems to provide the basis for reconstructing the prehistoric. Cooney reviews models of Neolithic settlement in Ireland, noting that distant origins of both dispersed and nucleated settlement patterns have been claimed (Cooney 2000: 68-9) and stressing that 'these scenarios of very long-term continuity grossly oversimplify the complexity and dynamism of settlement patterns and ignore the need to set them in particular social and historical contexts'.

75

The need for context and detail in our understanding of prehistoric settlement is also demonstrated by considering evidence for Early Neolithic settlement in Ireland and Scotland. Recent work on the dating of Neolithic archaeology in Britain and Ireland has provided considerably sharper resolution to some parts of our chronological data, and this has transformed some of our questions about settlement. In particular, it is now very clear that one of the earliest phases of the Neolithic in Ireland was characterized by the construction of (mainly) small, timber-framed houses (see Fig. 11). These houses have been found in great numbers in recent archaeological work (driven by modern infrastructure development), with more than 80 now known, and a distribution that covers most of the island, with most of the gaps likely to relate to the absence of recent excavations (for synthesis, see Smyth 2006, 2010). The timber houses have been subject to detailed dating programmes and appear to have had a very short period of use, perhaps only some 100-150 years. They appear to form one aspect of a suite of new material culture, buildings and practices of the Early Neolithic proper in Ireland. Associated palaeo-environmental and archaeobotanical evidence demonstrates categorically that farming was a central feature of the subsistence of the communities that inhabited these buildings (see also Cooney 2000). Most are found as isolated structures, although some are in small clusters, sometimes with evidence of enclosure. These timber buildings, often simply shorthanded as 'Neolithic houses', have recently been analysed by Jessica Smyth, who suggests that they demonstrate how society was organized around the central metaphor of the house. Construction and demolition of these buildings appears to have been ritualized, at least some of the time, including formal deposition of materials in association with construction and with repeated patterns of destruction and burning being very common. As such, and developing the arguments of Cooney (2000), Smyth proposes that the Early Neolithic communities of Ireland were 'house societies', where fundamental concepts of genealogy and relatedness, with all of the attendant implica-

3. Farming and the origins of villages

11. Early Neolithic house, Corbally, Co. Kildare, Ireland, excavated during development of quarry visible to rear.

tions for notions of property, belonging, and identity, were structured around the house (Smyth 2006, 2010). We assume also that production was fundamentally structured around the household. The emphasis on the house as a structuring principle of early Neolithic life in Ireland, reminds us that the distribution of settlement across the landscape is generated through the playing out of the dispositions and strategies of prehistoric agents: thus the peculiar settlement density of PPNB megasites may, in some ways, arise from repeated manifestations of expectations about appropriate levels of proximity to one's neighbours.

In contrast, in some parts of Scotland the construction of very large timber halls took place at the same time in the Early Neolithic period as the generally smaller, and clearly related houses were being constructed in Ireland. The Early Neolithic of Scotland and Ireland in general are comparable, sharing many new traditions of material culture. The large timber halls appear to play an important role in the agricultural landscape of Early Neolithic Scotland, but current interpretations suggest that they do not reflect a 'house society' in the same way. The function of these buildings remains a little unclear: possible roles as communal structures, such as 'big-men's houses', are sometimes advanced (see review in Brophy 2007), reminding us once more of the variation possible in organizing societies, although some still advocate a more domestic function (Murray, Murray & Fraser 2009). In any case, morphological features of these buildings are replicated in funerary monuments, and it appears that in Scotland aspects of the metaphorical qualities of this architecture were being utilized in different ways than in Ireland, regardless of whether the halls were houses or not. The principles that were generating settlement again appear to be different, even though the material forms are very similar. Our pictures of Neolithic settlement are drawn from specific places and contexts, and should not necessarily be extended to other areas in precisely the same form.

3. Farming and the origins of villages

The origin of things: rural romances

While emphasizing the importance of villages in our understanding of farming, we still like to maintain ideas of a rural idyll. They can be seen as all-pervasive, from children's picture books which emphasize traditional farming practices, to national parks, thatched cottages and farmers' markets, or even to putting pictures of individual farmers on pre-packed chicken breast in supermarkets, with descriptions of just how nice a life they and their animals lead. Michael Pollan (2006: 138) has discussed the important role that 'supermarket pastoral' (pastoral is itself an interesting word in this context) plays in the marketing of food, especially organic, free range and whole foods. A marketing representative of the US health-food chain, Whole Foods, explains that their use of imagery and language on packaging and other promotional materials aims to provide the consumer of organic foods with 'authentic experience … a return to a utopian past' in the hope that 'people will come together through organic foods to get back to the origin of things'. While much modern organic farming is in reality very big business, images of small-scale agriculture, of origins and utopia, are combined here with the influence of late capitalism. Stereotypes of villages and rural landscapes form an important element in colouring our image of the early Neolithic – the origin of things. From the images we have of farming, and from the anachronistic use of modern terms to describe early farming societies, we inevitably produce a Neolithic that is sharply differentiated from early Holocene societies, and consequently one in which the gulf between pre-farming and farming societies is hugely exaggerated.

The Natufian, for example, is still widely understood as a time when people began to settle down, develop a more sophisticated economy, and show increasing signs of social complexity. Natufian society has even been described as 'proto-' agricultural – literally 'first' or 'earliest form of'. In keeping with this description, Natufian settlements are often described as villages, with the smaller ones as hamlets. As noted above, while 'village' has a simple, technical meaning, it and 'hamlet' also carry powerful modern associations, many of which are captured by Pollan's notion of 'supermarket pastoral' and it is little surprise to see them related to discussions of the origins of agriculture.

Various aspects of this model, deep-seated as it is, have been criticized. To begin with, it is clear that the Natufian does not just suddenly appear as a new form of society in this region, 'complex from its inception' (Belfer-Cohen & Bar-Yosef 2000). It has clear roots in the early Epipalaeolithic of the Levant, especially as seen at the remarkable site of Ohalo II, dated to *c*. 23,000 calibrated years BP (Nadel 2004). It is remarkable in a southwest Asian context for its organic preservation, but possibly represents a much more common lifestyle than had been previously imagined. Here there are shelters made from organic materials and most importantly there is evidence for the substantial use of wild cereals, suggesting that we should not see their adoption in the late Epipalaeolithic Natufian as a radical economic change. Similarly, other forms of Natufian behaviour can be seen to grow out of an early Epipalaeolithic context, where sites have produced evidence for structures or burial practices. The Natufian, far from representing 'first farmers', comes to be seen as part of a longer story of changing hunter-gatherer lifestyles.

Change, as we have already argued, does not imply directionality, and the Natufian is itself not a simple reflection of the march of progress. Almost all synthetic discussions of the process of neolithization focus on the Early Natufian, when there does indeed appear to be evidence of some increasing sedentism. Unfortunately, the role of the Natufian as an orderly step is undermined by evidence for the Later Natufian and its terminal manifestations, the Final Natufian and the Harifian (see Chapter 4 for detailed discussion). These show an apparent increase in mobility and a decrease in settlement size, which appear to be adaptations to the climate change associated with the Younger Dryas.

Far from being a rural landscape in progressive (if interrupted) evolution, the very idea of villages and hamlets appears flawed. Very few Natufian sites show any real signs of a greatly increased degree of sedentism, such as structures and burials. Olszewski (1991) has noted that the number of sites with these features is only three for the whole of the Early Natufian, and six for the allegedly more mobile Late Natufian, not many for a period lasting 3,000 years. Other sites simply have thicker layers of occupation deposits, and Olszewski has argued convincingly that most of the larger sites would be perceived better as hunter-gatherer 'base camps', possibly visited frequently, but fitting this logistic role, rather than that of 'villages'. Bar-Yosef (1998) has also pointed out that the evidence for storage in the Natufian, often taken to be a key feature of Natufian developments, is almost non-existent. The evidence available is of a small number of pits of uncertain function. They are often referred to in a highly imaginative way as 'silos', which reflects an assumed harvest storage role. This assumption has then been used to deduce not only crop surpluses, but also collective storage and a whole new type of social structure. Oslzewski notes that, even if we accept their function, they are small, and appear more likely to relate to individual structures rather than to reflect a corporate project. In reality, their function remains speculative, and the conventional interpretation is more in accord with what our model of the Natufian tells us they *should* be (i.e. a proto-agricultural society, who must be on their way to living in villages), than what they really *are*. It is only in the PPNA that there is any incontrovertible evidence for storage, and it is associated with the harvesting of wild seeds. All too often, our preconceptions of what one should find in a familiar agricultural landscape colour reports of what we do find, when we attempt to discover the origins of that landscape.

Discussion

We began this chapter by outlining the common assumption that the Neolithic revolution lay at the origin of urban societies, especially through the foundation of large sedentary villages. Then, we hope, we deconstructed the idea of any necessary link between the presence of early farming communities and the presence of a farming village. Early agricultural communities organized themselves spatially in complex and variable ways. Sometimes this involved nucleation, at other times and in other places it did not. We must also note that similar physical structures can mean very different things. When nucleation *is* present, its social implications are not clear. Even settlements that involve many people living in one place do not necessarily appear to be anything that we would recognize as a village, nor the origin point of an unbroken historical trajectory to the modern village. Avoiding using the term 'village' is not a matter of academic pedantry, while in common parlance it may now be used for a small group of houses, and no longer require certain attributes such as a church, one of the issues we are arguing is against the use of a comfortable, familiar modern terminology to describe something so different to contemporary settlements. It is the hidden meaning and its baggage that is the biggest problem, and the use of village helps to preserve the identification of hunter-gatherers as 'other', and farmers as being like us. The way authors slip rapidly into highly dubious concepts such as the timeless Oriental village and European peasants reminds us how deep-seated these hidden meanings are.

We do not mean to deny a link between the appearance of farming and the ultimate rise of truly urban societies. Such societies are demonstrably founded on surpluses and on the social hierarchies which probably could not have arisen in most areas of the world without agricultural food production, and the accumulation and redistribution of wealth that it allowed. At the same time, we should not assume that this particular trajectory towards urbanism, even if it was encountered in different regions, is co-extensive with the appearance of agriculture, nor that it is any way an inevitable outcome of agriculture. The examples we have cited here demonstrate that alternative histories are possible, and that the choice of organization was central. This is important – all too often discussions

3. Farming and the origins of villages

of the 'origins of things' become teleological, by allowing parts to stand in for wholes. A fuller discussion of the relationship between agriculture and urbanization, and of the role of the 'village', must incorporate the human diversity demonstrated by archaeology and to consider the different ways in which settlements can be organized. At the same time, a consideration of this diversity brings into sharp focus the importance of particular historical agencies in shaping the world, whether they turned out to be the beginnings of things that followed, or ways of organizing people in time and space that have no current analogues.

4

Progressing, unequally, to agriculture

After the agricultural revolution, in most trajectories of
development, we see the development of communities
with leaders and followers, where the high ranks often
became hereditary. (Renfrew 2007: 160)

The emergence of agriculture is often explicitly linked to a
supposed change from egalitarian to hierarchical societies. In
association with sedentism, a rise in the production, storage
and exchange of material goods enabled the rise of hierarchy,
variously presented as a terrible side effect of the new ways of
living, as a benefit in terms of social organization, or as an
innate human tendency. This chapter explores these themes of
equality and hierarchy. We begin by examining the nature of
'egalitarian' hunter-gatherers.

The social relationships of hunting and gathering communities are often collapsed into the distinction between simple and
complex hunter-gatherers. We revisit aspects of our earlier
accounts here, emphasizing the teleology that is often implied
in linking complex hunter-gatherers with 'pre-adaptations' to
agriculture. We also emphasize the role of research traditions
in constructing narratives of change over time. Throughout,
there is a concern that the construction of synthetic accounts in
the past has relied too greatly on simplifications of the real
variability.

4. Progressing, unequally, to agriculture

The origins of inequality

As noted above, many recent accounts associate the origin of the Neolithic with the rise of inequality in human societies. These accounts are underpinned by an assumption that hunter-gatherer societies were egalitarian, with little or no inequality present. For example, McCarter (2007: 121-2) provides the demonstrably false line of thought that '... everywhere in the world, hunter-gatherer social systems are egalitarian ... individual members of a band aren't interested in power ... Resources, especially food, are pooled and shared without keeping track of who gave the most (or least)'. Renfrew (2007: 160 and passim) sees the emergence of inequality as one of the 'mysteries of prehistory', associating it with a stage in the development of humanity when people begin to ascribe value to material goods, so enabling their possessors to be associated with particular positions in society. For Renfrew, this development happens at the same time as the rise of sedentism and the agricultural revolution. What both these authors are doing, as is so often the case, is presenting modern simple hunter-gatherers as the origin point from which a development takes place. Our discussion here will concentrate on two points. First, we will suggest that the common association of egalitarian society with hunter-gatherers is not as simple as is sometimes implied, and secondly, we will take a slightly longer perspective when we examine the nature of egalitarian societies.

Although hunter-gatherers are frequently described as egalitarian, the reality is much more complicated. Complex hunter-gatherer societies that were not egalitarian included people such as the Kwakiutl of the northwest coast of North America. They lived in large permanent settlements, possessed slaves, had hereditary rulers, sought prestige, and utilized extensive redistributions of wealth (the famous 'potlatches'). Some authors have seen these complex hunter-gatherers as the products of particular environmental conditions, with abundant resources, which provided many of the conditions

85

otherwise experienced by sedentary farmers. However, Robert Kelly (1995: 293-331) points out that archaeologists are finding evidence for these kinds of hunter-gatherers in many different environments. He suggests that a key challenge would be to understand the relationship between environment and variability within the non-egalitarian hunter-gatherer category. As we have previously noted, other writers suggest that the 'egalitarian' character of some contemporary hunter-gatherers is an adaptive strategy, which they have developed to compensate for the very marginal conditions in which they now live in the modern world. This argument suggests that egalitarian hunter-gathering is a product of recent history, not an origin point, and should not be the basis for all comparisons with prehistory.

The archaeological record of the Upper Palaeolithic, for example, suggests that some very ancient hunter-gatherers appear to have exhibited hierarchy and status. To take but one example, the remarkable Upper Palaeolithic burials at Sungir include a man buried with nearly 3,000 ivory beads attached to his clothes, as well as 25 mammoth ivory bracelets, pierced animal teeth and other paraphernalia. A teenage male (12-14 years old) and a young female (9-10) were buried together, with exceptionally rich grave goods, including about 5,000 beads each. Replication work has suggested that these bead assemblages represent thousands of hours of labour. Any interpretation of the status of an individual when he or she was alive, from grave goods placed with the dead, is difficult. These exceptional burials, for example, may have been enriched by mourning gifts, indicating not the status of the dead, but the scale of the extended family that grieved for them. However, the presence of very wealthy burials of young individuals is often supposed to indicate some form of inherited status, the argument being that they could not have achieved high influence in their communities through their own activities, but are likely to have gained some stature from being related to influential people. The Sungir burials, therefore, cannot conclusively demonstrate hierarchy in the Upper Palaeolithic, but they do at least indicate the ability to accumulate and dispose of wealth, one of the key prerequisites for establishing and contesting hierarchies.

Accepting that many hunter-gatherers are clearly not egalitarian, it is still important for us to examine social relationships within so-called egalitarian hunter-gatherer societies in more detail. Kelly (1995: 296) stresses that '[Egalitarian] does not mean that all members have the same amount of goods, food, prestige, or authority. Egalitarian societies are not those in which everyone is equal, or in which everyone has equal amounts of material goods, but those in which everyone has equal access to food, to the technology needed to acquire resources, and to the paths leading to prestige.' Key mechanisms to stop people turning temporary influence into power include ridicule and ostracism. There is considerable debate about the nature of gender relationships within 'egalitarian' hunter-gatherer societies. Some commentators state that men do have greater influence than women (e.g. Kelly 1995; Endicott 1999 for an alternative view). The supposition that food is given freely and with no return has been criticized. An alternative model suggests that successful hunting of large game by men is a signal of status, and leads to reproductive benefits – for an extensive discussion, see Gurven and Hill (2009). All of this suggests that, rather than demonstrating that humans are not interested in power, egalitarian societies have found a way of managing a human tendency towards hierarchy. Based on his review of egalitarian hunter-gatherers, Kelly (p. 296) stresses that 'the maintenance of an egalitarian society requires effort. Egalitarian relations do not come easily; they are not the natural results of the absence of stratification.' These conclusions give further credence to the suggestion that egalitarian societies should not be considered as points from which development takes place.

We can extend this argument by taking a longer evolutionary perspective. In their *Baboon Metaphysics* (2007), Dorothy Cheney and Robert Seyfarth examine the social and intellectual life of baboons, on the basis of long-term fieldwork in the

Okavango Delta in Botswana. These baboons inhabit a social world that is exceptionally hierarchical; baboons must recognize social hierarchies, including complex changes in hierarchies and inherited roles. Set against this, they make short-term decisions about mating and friendship, as well as managing long-term relationships. The result, the authors claim, is an intricate social drama that would be familiar to readers of Jane Austen. Hierarchies are strong in gorillas and both species of chimpanzees, which are all genetically closer to us than baboons, and bonobos also show gender variability in social hierarchies. The idea that most primates are innately hierarchical rather than egalitarian has clear implications for the origins or status of hierarchy amongst humans. Cheney and Seyfarth describe a visit in the field from a member of the British Royal family who upon being told that hierarchy and rank, including inherited status, were central to baboon life replied: 'I always knew ... that when people who aren't like us claim that hereditary rank is not part of human nature they must be wrong. Now you've given me evolutionary proof!' (Cheney & Seyfarth 2007: 74-5).

Taking a broader view of the origins of inequality therefore presents some challenges to the idea that hunter-gatherers represent the egalitarian origin point from which agriculture separated us. The broader context says that humans, in common with many of their evolutionary relatives, have innate tendencies to hierarchy and that many recent hunter-gatherer ways of life succeeded in managing to live with them. The assumption that the Neolithic revolution is the origin point for the development of inequality is therefore deeply flawed. On the one hand, it fails to recognize significant variation in the social organization of hunter-gatherers past and present, and all too often appears to misunderstand what 'egalitarian' might actually mean. On the other hand, it appears that egalitarianism was not a state of nature, or a zero point, from which the history of political relationships could develop. We simply do not know to what extent egalitarianism characterized early human societies, and we must not assume its presence. Egalitarianism may even have been a central historical achievement of early human societies, and its loss would then require more detailed and nuanced consideration than models of revolution allow.

The complex hunter-gatherer and the inevitability of farming

As noted in Chapter 1, many discussions of the transition to agriculture use the twin stereotypes of simple and complex hunter-gatherers. The complex hunter-gatherer society is found more frequently in archaeological than in anthropological research. Price and Brown (1985) thought that such societies were more likely to appear in the late Pleistocene or early Holocene than earlier. There are classic examples in the literature, the Natufian of the Levant and the Ertebølle of southern Scandinavia. They play opposite roles in the narratives, the former group being pre-adapted to agriculture and sedentism, which gave them an unstable transitional role, while the latter represented a highly evolved hunter-gatherer solution that was stable and resistant to farming. Rowley-Conwy (2001) has presented a strong case, using Arctic Inuit examples, where there was no possibility of farming ever developing, to show that the so-called complex hunter-gatherer society can emerge at any point and vanish again, all without any relation to agriculture, either transitional or resistant.

The best known example of a complex hunter-gatherer society in southwest Asia is the Natufian. The Natufian is routinely described as an unstable 'complex hunter-gatherer' society, bound to change to a fully fledged agricultural sedentary one when the right environmental pressures were imposed. In evolutionary terms the Natufian fills an important step between the simple hunter-gatherers of the Pleistocene and the farmers of the Holocene. But, as we have discussed, while in its early manifestation there is some evidence for increasing sedentism, increasing materiality and symbolic culture, and possibly the start of a change in relations with the world it is generally believed that with the deterioration of climate towards the end of the Pleistocene, especially in the Younger Dryas, this way of life became unsustainable and that there was a return to a simple hunter-gatherer life-style with the Late Natufian. The Late Natufian is not so frequently discussed as the early Natufian, and indeed in synthetic accounts the Late is often collapsed into the Early. For any standard evolutionary approach to archaeology, this is a necessary way to deal with the problem, that instead of moving forward to the Neolithic stage, the Late Natufian shows many signs of going backwards.

One of the best studied facets of the Late Natufian comes from the Negev desert. It is a variation which has been thought to be such a specific adaptation to local conditions that it has been given the distinctive name Harifian, after the highlands of the HaHarif. Goring-Morris (1987) provides a detailed account of how Harifian society made use of the markedly vertical topography of the area, to develop a way of moving up and down hill depending on the season – mobile, but sophisticated. Their life-style enabled them to survive in an area that was subsequently abandoned, until climate improved again during the PPNB. This temporarily very successful adaptation had one apparent fault. It did not appear to be on the main track to agriculture, and indeed is often described in somewhat pejorative terms, being but a short lived attempt at an adaptation (Belfer-Cohen & Bar-Yosef 2000), or a society that did not cross the threshold to farming (Goring-Morris 1987) and which in the end simply faded away. The Harifian serves in fact as an example of how the early Natufian was not a direct, one way, linear route to the Neolithic. As climate changed the Natufian as whole altered and adapted. In the Harif the adaptation was significant, and showed how it was possible for a complex hunter-gatherer society to go in an alternative direction.

To us, the Harifian is fascinating, because it provides a very clear example of one of a whole array of specific social and economic adaptations in the late Epipalaeolithic, a period that was not really dominated by societies clearly *en route* to the

12. Locus 3 complex at Ramat Harif (G8), a typical late Pleistocene Harifian site in south-west Asia, incorporating a stone shelter and a grinding tool fixed in the floor.

Neolithic. At the same time, there is some evidence that the Harifian may actually be more closely connected than other socie- ties are, to subsequent groups in the region. Its material culture is partly characterized by the presence of flint points, one of the first manifestations of what becomes an important tool class both in the PPNA (especially the el-Khiam notched point) and in the many PPNB forms. Although scholars working on the Harifian have tended to emphasize its isolation, a number of Harifian sites contain el-Khiam points. Intriguingly, it is possible that as we find out more about the PPNA of southern Jordan, east of the HaHarif, until recently seen as equally marginal, we are beginning to see signs that the Harifian provides a very good local context for PPNA developments. This is most visible when we compare architectural forms. For example, the earliest PPNA architecture at WF16 (Finlayson & Mithen 2007) is very similar to that found at the Harifian sites. (See Fig. 12 for an example of typical hunter-gatherer Harifian architecture.)

Points of origin

Social evolutionary theories not only incorporate developmental sequences, but are also implicitly linked to origins research. Origins research has, of course, been very significant in the development of research into the Neolithic. Much of it continues to this day to seek for the beginning of the period – the first signs of animal or plant domestication, the first appearance of true sedentism, or indeed of the village – with the potential academic and public acclaim of finding the first, the earliest, the original, being a key driver of research. Origins research has its own problems (see Gamble 2007 for an extended discussion), but there have been additional factors that have taken it into strange directions, when it concerns itself with the transition from hunting and gathering to farming. Part of its peculiarity may relate to sacred geography, the association of the fall of Adam and Eve with the Neolithic revolution, with the location of Eden in Mesopotamia, and with ideas of the fertile crescent as *the* point of origin (see Smail 2007, and discussion of his ideas in our Introduction). There is also the direct link with regions that contain the wild progenitors of domesticated species, and the assumption that these must be key areas in the story of domestication. The areas targeted for much early research were both informed by these ideas and informed them, leading to a dense concentration of research in the southern Levant, in the northern Levant around the upper Euphrates, and in the so called hilly flanks of the fertile crescent. The database from these areas remains extraordinarily rich, although hopefully we are becoming more aware that this is in part being seen as especially true simply with regard to places where fieldwork has been conducted. New areas, especially in central Turkey, have increasingly come to the fore as fieldwork proceeds.

The identification of the Natufian in the southern Levant, or more particularly the identification of the early Natufian, has for a long time led people to presume, especially following the work of Ofer Bar-Yosef, that for the earliest developments this small area was critical. How this then plays out becomes a fascinating study in archaeological approaches, and indeed in the tendency of archaeologists to assume that their own field research area is central. Bar-Yosef, and those who follow him, tend to argue that in the Late Natufian, its culture spreads, from what they describe as the 'Natufian homeland' in the south, to the north, to include sites on the Euphrates. A second approach is shown by Moore, the excavator of Abu Hureyra, one of the best known early sites in this northern Levantine region, who claims that there are sufficient points of difference for the material in the north to be given a different assignation. Delage (2004) has convincingly pointed out that there is a third school of thought, the 'Lyons School', based on French work. This was enormously influenced by François Hours, whose background was in history, and who brought with him ideas from Braudel and the *Annales* school, most particularly about the roots of Western civilization around the Mediterranean, and of there having been centres of innovation which moved over time, from Mesopotamia to Egypt, to Greece and then Rome, and so on to the Renaissance. The model is very much set within an eighteenth-century enlightenment progressive paradigm that sees Western civilization as the peak of development. This intellectual framework has directed much French Neolithic research. It includes the concept that the Natufian in the south was crucial for the first stage of the Neolithic, and that the focus of innovation then moved north to the Upper Euphrates. The idea of progress that it incorporates is very specific – the importance of the Neolithic transition in southwest Asia is that it provides the subsistence package for subsequent Western civilization (cf. Aurenche & Kozlowski 1999). Areas outside the centres of innovation become clearly marginal, both in terms of their failure to move forward, and in being academically less interesting.

In a loose sense this sort of framework has governed much research, although its French manifestation is clearer than other ones. It is inherently suited to the quest for firsts and origins. Delage (2004: 106) has also made the point that archaeological literature tends to assume that whenever any trait has been invented which is 'found valuable in reference to modern western civilization, [it] will always be kept and passed on from one generation to another in the same group or civilization, and from one civilization to another'. This habit plays a part in the backward attribution of traits, in terms such as 'proto-agriculture', or the belief that PPNB megasites were in some way early expressions of urbanism, as for example in Frick (1997), or Simmons and Najjar (2004). It also helps to explain why so few synthetic accounts attempt to deal with the extremely variable nature of the archaeological record.

The Natufian is especially important to this debate, because this is when people are believed to leave nature and move to culture, but, as noted above, there is little discussion of the way in which much of the Late Natufian shows a return to greater mobility and smaller communities. Later on, although there is much discussion of the megasite collapse, there is no recognition that this revealed that PPNB settlement patterns were a unique form, which did not evolve into urban or even village sites. The overall model assumes that there must be progress and so, to achieve it, jumps from area to area. The most extreme jump is at the start of the Epipalaeolithic, when the centre of human evolution was seen to move from the west European Magdalenian to the Near East (Cauvin 1987, see also Lewis-Williams & Pearce 2005 for similar arguments), but all of them require a rather discontinuous process of development. What they do provide is a very straightforward move towards a grand synthesis, as it is only by focusing on the centres, of which there is only one at any given moment, that the overall narrative can be found, ready to be recounted.

It is only very recently that this type of model has been challenged by the suggestion that it is the overall region that is important, that the region we need to focus on may be much larger than was previously conceived (cf. Barker 2006), and that it is not homogeneous (Gebel 2004). Then it is the mosaic of interacting communities that is significant, not the changes at any one locale. An extremely important aspect of this new viewpoint is that it no longer marginalizes most of the evidence. In particular, we no longer have to dismiss some groups as being unfit to cross the threshold to the Neolithic; interactions become allowable between contemporary groups, regardless of their subsistence base and degree of sedentism, much as in the modern world; and the strictly developmental sequence from hunter-gatherer to farmer becomes less mandatory. Indeed, we are required to envisage a Late Pleistocene-Early Holocene world in which there are connections between different communities and their subsistence bases. All this takes us back to the question of what an archaeological culture really is, or to put it another way, are material-culture variations that just reflect subsistence variations necessarily significant in themselves?

Discussion

The relations between inequality and the consequences of agriculture are important. The modern world is characterized by gross inequality, and an understanding of the trajectories that have led to this situation is greatly to be desired. But to collapse 'hunter-gatherer' and 'farmer' respectively into 'egalitarian' and 'hierarchical', as has been done in many synthetic accounts, is demonstrably problematic. Not all hunter-gatherers are 'egalitarian' in the precise sense implied by the term, and the looser associations that the label carries are not at all helpful. It is not clear that the original state of human social organization was egalitarian, nor indeed that *any* 'original state' is at all relevant to discussing events at the time of the transition to agriculture, many tens of thousands of years after the appearance of modern humans. As so often, it appears that these accounts are heavily influenced by the modern political context from which they arise.

As discussed in our Introduction, accounts of revolution are underpinned by notions of progress, and the problems this can cause are well demonstrated by discussions of hunter-gatherer societies in Europe as being 'preadapted' to agriculture – as having traits that made the transition to agriculture easy for these communities. Preadaptation is a concept that is commonly evoked in the late Epipalaeolithic archaeology of southwest Asia, leading to categories such as 'proto-agriculturalists'. In the context of narratives about the development of features of a society preadaptation is clearly evolutionary in tone, but as Sterelny and Griffiths (1999: 219) comment, this 'terminology is very misleading. The word *preadaptation* suggests that evolution is forward-looking – anticipating the future needs of the organism. Evolution by natural selection cannot look forward because it cannot occur costs in anticipation of later benefits.' Without entering into an extensive debate about whether social evolution takes place according to the same structures as biological evolution, it is clear that the concept of preadaptation is directional and is clearly associated with some of the teleological aspects of origins narratives that we have been discussing here, Gould and Vrba (1982) developed the notion of 'exaptation' to describe traits that had been adapted to suit one form but ended up being used for something else. Sterelny and Griffiths, however, consider that because secondary adaptations – a trait being retained in different circumstances because it can serve a different function – are very common, and distinction between exaptation and adaptation is not useful: 'the important distinction is between all the selection processes and the processes that are happening today, but have played no role in past evolution' (1999: 220). Again the emphasis is on understanding the relationship between particular traits and the particular demands they face at an particular time. This requires understanding both their original role and how they relate to new processes.

Progress and origins also play a part in the selectivity that is employed in synthetic accounts. We have shown how the very interesting Harifian adaptation is overtly ruled out of the discussion of transition, while other aspects of the contemporary Late Natufian are more quietly forgotten. We could take instead more inclusive approaches that would consider earlier developments, from the so-called 'human revolution' of the

4. Progressing, unequally, to agriculture

Upper Palaeolithic, to the very gradual developments in economy and society that we can track through the entire Epipalaeolithic, or we could increase the geographical spread of the context in which changes are taking place, as proposed by Barker (2006). Painting such a larger picture certainly still helps to make those periods appear less visible, in which a steady progressive evolution is interrupted, such as the Late Natufian or the PPNB megasite collapse. However, we would suggest that they do remain significant, as reflections of human history that have actually taken place, and are indications of how diversity is an important part of a process that is not linear.

5

The Neolithic mind

Thus it may be said that the first people to be fully
human, to share the humanity that is common to human
societies in the world today, came into existence at the
beginning of the Neolithic in southwest Asia. And the
success of their new ideas, new ideology and new symbols
was the foundation on which was built their rapid expansion and wide-spread adoption. (Watkins 2005: 84)

Increasing interest in cognitive archaeology has led to suggestions (see e.g. Renfrew 2003, Watkins 2004) that the Neolithic
is the final evolutionary event that leads to modern people and
that in some (generally rather unspecified) way, people were
not fully human before the Neolithic. This chapter explores
these issues, concentrating mainly on the arguments, first for a
cognitive revolution associated with sedentism, and second for
the development of religion and symbolism both taking place at
the same time as the origins of agriculture. Both are founded
on supposedly new material conditions that came into being at
this time, and as discussed in Chapter 4, some writers have
also connected these new possibilities with the increasing evidence for hierarchy and status – concepts that are associated in
turn with the development of notions of property.

Our first discussion centres on the supposed cognitive
revolution created by the inhabitation of an increasingly
'built' and 'artificial' environment. We suggest that this
model does not do justice to the ways in which inhabitation
of landscapes by non-agriculturalists encompasses practical
and symbolic routines. We then consider the supposition

that the origins of religion and transformation of symbols are to be found at this time.

A cognitive revolution

Trevor Watkins (2005) and Colin Renfrew (2007) have both argued that the Neolithic involved a cognitive revolution, related to the changing requirements of living in a large-scale sedentary society. To us, the most surprising aspect of these stimulating discussions is that these writers contend that in many ways the hunter-gatherers who preceded the Neolithic were not fully human, and would not have been recognizably human to us, whereas the farmers of the Neolithic would have been. Given our emphasis in this book on the fact that the concept of hunter-gatherer is, and always has been, a way of dividing the modern, Western 'us' from a spatially or temporally separated 'other', it should be no surprise that we find this argument problematic and suspect that some long-standing stereotypes are helping to support it.

Central support for the idea that there was a cognitive revolution is found in the supposition that early farmers lived in the constructed space of early farming villages, and the perception that this constructed space is a radical departure from what preceded it. As Watkins (2009: 648) puts it 'Because we are familiar from earliest infancy with the experience of living in large communities in built environments, we may have difficulty in recognizing the novelty of such a way of life, and the challenges that it presented to societies who confronted it for the first time.' We will return to this important point.

Watkins's proposition ties together increasing sedentism, population density and changing materiality, in a variety of cognitive frames. His basic contention is that living in large groups for extended periods of time is unusual in the long term of human history and that this experience of proximity places particular cognitive demands on individuals. Following Merlin Donald (e.g. 1991), Watkins argues for the significance of 'external symbolic storage systems' (ESSS). They are to be seen as aspects of material culture that embody and encode particular ways of understanding the world, and in this model, facilitate the engagement of individuals with the problems of proximity and information. ESSS are said to allow for greater cognitive complexity amongst people, as providing material prompts for action, and further potential possibilities for social performances of different kinds. Watkins suggests that the architecture of the first villages is best understood as a fundamentally symbolic built environment – that this architecture is in itself an ESSS, and that this is the first *artificial* environment. As individuals grow up in these environments they learn to negotiate and engage with the mass of symbolic complexity that surrounds them, and indeed to use this new ability to negotiate their way through the social networks, of varying scales, that enable them to deal with the problem of living in such proximity to other individuals. The inhabitants of these large settlements are developing their cognitive abilities in a radically different environment from that of hunter-gatherers – it is significantly more complex – and the inhabitants themselves can therefore be seen to be different. It is central here that the difference is not simply one of scale, or quantity of cognitive activity, but of quality; the entire cognitive relationship is different. Renfrew (2007) offers a very similar proposition, in terms of 'material engagement theory' and the role assumed by the 'distributed mind' with the appearance of sedentism. He writes (p. 135) that 'the most decisive turn in prehistory ... came with the order-of-magnitude increase in the varieties of engagement between humans and the material world, mediated by the use of symbols, that began with the development of sedentism' – sedentism itself being enabled by agriculture. Renfrew claims in particular that this must be the moment when modern humanity emerges, and that the lack of progress before this time, despite the richness of the Upper Palaeolithic, downgrades the importance of the first appearance of *Homo sapiens,* when it comes to considering the real human revolution.

Hodder (2005) has also developed some of these ideas, sug-

100

gesting that the increased materiality of sedentary societies led to a greater *entanglement*. He recognizes that objects had acquired symbolic power at least by the Upper Palaeolithic, and tries to see what might have changed at the start of the Neolithic. He looks at how the process of making things becomes more socially complex, requiring a network of entanglements, both in material things and in social relations. As the things that are made become more complex and more numerous, the web of networks extends. In particular, the durability of the new objects extends the range of reciprocal exchanges and helps to enable accumulation. Exchange of durable objects allows exchange to be remembered through the object. Hodder connects this perception to the ideas of Woodburn (1982) about 'delayed-return' economies (both hunter-gatherer and farmer) in which the return on efforts or exchanges may be long term, requiring social institutions to be better developed. We note that the important point here is not the nature of the economy in general, but the possession of durable goods for exchange.

These interesting proposals require careful consideration. We have already suggested that the connection between the Neolithic revolution and the development of villages or other forms of large-scale settlement requires reappraisal, but we will not pursue this discussion further now, other than to note that the one phenomenon does not presuppose the other and they do not go together in all locations. Here we focus on whether the ideas that the nature of the engagement, or the character of architecture as an ESSS are really such dramatic transformations as these proposals imply.

Watkins (2009a: 647) claims that it was only the Epipalaeolithic, and especially the Neolithic, that brought the construction of 'architecture as opposed to the simple construction of shelters'. Both he and Renfrew are here broadly following the idea of Peter Wilson (1988) that the adoption of the house as a central organizing principle of society is in great distinction to the usage of hunters and gatherers, who are considered to live mainly in the open spaces around and between their structures – which they do not see as 'houses'.

This view appears to overstate the distinction. One could cite numerous examples of buildings long pre-dating the Epipalaeolithic that embody complex symbolic understandings of the environment – such as, for example, the mammoth skull and tusk huts of Mezhirich in the Ukraine (*c.* 15,000 years ago). In southwest Asia, structures appear only occasionally before the late Epipalaeolithic, but when they do, they almost immediately seem to include buildings with special features, suggesting some communal or ceremonial purpose. There are serious problems in assuming a simple connection between greater architectural permanence and either sedentism or indeed the development of a 'house' or 'home'. A review of the literature on contemporary hunter-gatherer or nomadic pastoral societies demonstrates that mobile dwellings can provide a fundamentally symbolic reference point for communities. David Anderson (2006), for example, discusses how, in Evenki lodges, there was a social ideal of a circular space which was conceived as a corridor wrapped around a hearth, with particular locations assigned to particular roles (men, women, guests) at particular times. Movement was highly constrained, with, for example, a prohibition on circling through the corridor, and directions being given for entrance and egress. Anderson notes the similarities between these social structures in Canada and Russia, and a wider literature emphasizes the importance of the symbolism of the fire and the making of offerings to the spirits of the fire at the centre of the hearth. This architecture is not permanent in its material expression in any one place, but in its varied spatial manifestations it is considered the central point of the world, and its reconstruction is the basic grounding and centring of a society's inhabitation of a new location. In this way, its permanence lies in the relationships between components, and not in any given expression of those components. Anderson notes that this ideal is constantly renegotiated in different social conditions and that the structuring of space according to gender and other factors takes place across a 'camp' at a much broader scale than that frequently discussed archaeologically, implying that aspects of this structuring will be hard to identify archaeologically. To describe mobile or temporary architecture simply as 'shelter' does often seem to be erroneous. In contemporary southwest Asia, no one would argue that a Bedouin tent was not a 'home', while ethnography of the recent past shows that many of the substantial buildings associated with traditional villages were designed as secure stores, for communities that did not remain in one place all year round. This finding may be reflected in the prehistoric blocking of doors, notably at the MPPNB site of Shkarat Msaiad in southern Jordan where, despite the massive, sometimes multi-storeyed, architecture, the excavators have deduced that the site may have been occupied only on a seasonal basis. In his discussion of buildings and dwellings Ingold (2000) reviews Cribb's studies of tent dwellings and village houses in Turkey and Iran where 'despite differences in the building materials used and the flexibility they afford, the tent and the house were virtually identical in their underlying organizational templates. What really distinguished the house from the tent was the degree to which the imposed, cultural design – shared by villagers and nomads alike – is actually translated into enduring material structures' (Ingold 2000: 181). What is particularly important here is that villages are each established in one place and thus build upon existing physical forms, whereas nomadic pastoralists are mobile and each new occupation starts with a new space, but nevertheless repeats the physical form each time.

A further difficulty arises from our routine assumption that buildings are houses, and therefore represent homes. The very small size of PPNA structures (typically less than 3 m in their maximum dimension) and the frequent presence of internal features such as marked burials and built-in grinding tools and cutting slabs, suggests that much living must have been done in the areas between buildings, much as Wilson implies for hunter-gatherers. Similarly in the earlier PPNB, there is evidence suggesting that as the space between buildings shrank, roof space was used more often. It seems unlikely that the exact function of interior space was that of the multi-purpose living environment suggested by the term 'house'.

Apart from the building itself, the identification of ESSS in the past seems to require past existence to be vouched for by archaeological visibility. One might consider instead, for example, the symbolic landscapes inhabited by contemporary Australian Aboriginal communities. For these hunter-gatherers, the landscape was formed in the Dreamtime (that is both past and present) by the actions of the ancestors, by a combination of physical action and naming (or singing). Thus, particular hills are where ancestors lay down to rest, particular waterholes are where someone was using a digging stick, or particular veins of quartz are considered to be the semen of the ancestors. This richly symbolic landscape is central to Aboriginal existence, and can structure a variety of material practices. Thus in Western Arnhem Land quartz is considered to be the bones of an ancestor, and an especially suitable raw material for manufacturing hunting weapons, because it is shimmering and iridescent, which are considered magical properties (Taçon 1991). It is therefore quarried and exchanged over long distances. This kind of richly symbolic landscape is difficult to access archaeologically, but must surely be precisely the kind of all-encompassing ESSS discussed by Watkins. If ESSS embody and encode understandings of the world, themselves then generating further activity, then the landscape itself may be an ESSS and the appearance of architecture may not be such a radical disjuncture at all. In fact, the rapid appearance of special purpose buildings in the Natufian and PPNA may indicate that the ideas underlying these structures were already in place, before the structures were built in stone and mud.

One of the critical difficulties here is that little serious attention has been paid to understanding how hunter-gatherer cosmology structured material behaviour in southwest Asia – not least because of the nature of the evidence. Instead, too often, and as noted above, such discussions refer back to generalized hunter-gatherers, as for example when Lewis-Williams

and Pearce use Upper Palaeolithic cave art of Europe as a
'tentative' basis for speculation on 'Upper Palaeolithic and
Mesolithic cosmology in the Near East' (2005: 82). In contrast,
in northwest Europe several writers have suggested the basis
of Neolithic monumentality may lie in hunter-gatherer cosmology and the celebration of particular places (e.g. Cummings
2003, 2010) or how myth may have structured routine action
(Warren 2007).

Underpinning much of this debate about a cognitive revolution is the old opposition – between hunter-gatherers who live
in nature, and farmers who live in a built environment. Ingold
(2000) approaches Wilson's presentation of the distinction between the natural and the built environment through a broader
consideration of the notion of 'building' as a distinct interven-
tion in a natural world. He reviews the search for the 'first
building' that such a notion presupposes, taking account of the
fact that animals too clearly build structures, even if these are
not normally described as architectural (but see Gould & Gould
2007). Ingold (2000) thinks that searching for the first building,
on these lines, is misleading. Following Heidegger he suggests
that in order to build we must dwell. That is to say, that rather
than standing apart from the world and imposing design upon
it, our starting point is always embodied in and grounded on
whatever skills, projects and capabilities have been developed.
'Building then, is a process that is continually going on, for as
long as people dwell in an environment. It does not begin here,
with a pre-formed plan, and end there, with a finished artefact'
(p. 188). Similar reasoning is implied by the fields of developmental systems theory in biology, which Ingold draws on. They
suggest that all animals (including humans) are inevitably
embedded into fields of relationships with others and that their
very development as organisms is inseparable from this relationship between genetic and non-genetic information. To start
from the idea of *any* environment being *artificial* is to build on
a bad foundation. It is better just to accept that animals grow
into different environments and that they manipulate this situation in different ways. Gould and Gould (2007: 271) explain

how the processes of play and growth in an environment are central to any animal's ability to construct architecture. In fact, one of the key aspects of being human *may* be our remarkable ability to make different environments our homes, enabled by these processes of developmental growth. It may be difficult for us to imagine the cognitive strain involved in living in the first large settlements, but humans do live in all kinds of remarkable conditions. McGhee (2004: 49-50), for example, gives an account of the first colonizers of the high Arctic which includes a discussion of the Independence-Tuniit, of northern Greenland (*c.* 4,000 years BP) who may have passed the long Arctic winter in minimally heated simple tents, possibly in a state of semi-torpor. He concludes that 'at least some tribes of Tuniit accepted and learned to contend with living conditions beyond the range of those known to any peoples of the recent world'. See also McMillan and Yellowhorn (2004: 263ff.). Humans have lived, and do live, in all kinds of different environments which make all kinds of different demands on individuals. It seems problematic to separate out the 'built' environment as categorically different.

In order to understand the relationships between people and their environments we must look beyond buildings, and understand processes of inhabitation. Sometimes, as in the ethnographic examples we cite, these lead to particular kinds of temporary buildings, at other times to more permanent ones. We suggest that those who adhere to the cognitive revolution theory have at times failed to consider these processes in a hunter-gatherer context. These notions of architecture and ESSS can both be seen to downplay the complex ways in which hunter-gatherers structure their world. In fact, one could argue that both of them dehumanize past hunter-gatherers, by removing their capability for complex symbolic expression only in order to show that the appearance of this symbolic capability is evidence of a revolution that separates us from them. Much of our knowledge of the hunter-gatherer world view is recent, and the ethnographic detail now strengthens our assertions that symbolism is not the preserve of permanent buildings and portable material culture. Renfrew (2007) discusses the use of modern hunter-gatherer analogies, essentially arguing, as we do, that they are separated in time from Palaeolithic hunter-gatherers by many thousands of years, and that they have their own historical trajectories and their own understandings of the world. We agree in this, just as we agree with Renfrew's statement that 'we have no way of knowing the extent to which such systems (of engagement) had developed during the Paleolithic period' (p. 140). But we would suggest that the symbolic complexity of Upper Palaeolithic Art, say, or that of the burial traditions of this period, must make us assume that complex symbolic understandings existed, even if those may be difficult to reconstruct for particular times and places. Renfrew's desire to avoid bringing attributes of present hunter-gatherers into the past means that he is left with no clear sense of what past hunter-gatherers were. They therefore become the null point from which everything else develops.

Inverting arguments

Most of the accounts of the cognitive revolution associated with the Neolithic draw heavily on southwest Asian material, although they often make passing reference to comparative processes elsewhere. But in other parts of the world, the nature of the Neolithic is very different. One might therefore expect that any cognitive revolution that took place in association with the appearance of farming in these areas should also be different. To take northwest Europe as one example, there is considerable disagreement as to the extent of sedentary and especially aggregated settlement and some of the problems of dense urban living that lie at the heart of Watkins's and Renfrew's arguments would therefore appear to have been by-passed. And yet, in a strange inversion, it appears that the monuments that are characteristic of these regions (see Fig. 13), rather than the settlements of other regions, can themselves cause the same revolution. Renfrew (2007), for example, argues that 'the most important new social or institutional fact that emerges

13. Neolithic Passage Tomb at Loughcrew, Co. Meath, Ireland. Megalithic monuments are an iconic aspect of the Irish landscape.

from the reality of *living together in a village* like those of the early Neolithic of western Asia is the community of the inhabitants. From the association of living together, and from the daily interactions of the village street, come shared understandings' (p. 149, our emphasis). This in turn is seen as categorically different from the 'seasonal get-togethers' of mobile hunter-gatherer communities. In making the case for dispersed settlement in Neolithic Europe, and for early funerary monuments playing a role in bringing communities together for particular ceremonies and feasts (see Fig. 13 for an example), he discusses (p. 154) the 'new sense of community' displayed by these monuments; suggesting that 'the monument, like the village itself, can thus bring a new kind of social reality to the community that inhabits the locality ... the very process of construction of the village or of the monument in a sense calls that community into being' (p. 156). This is asking us to have our cake and eat it. On the one hand, temporary gatherings of hunter-gatherers, even if they involve intense ritual and social interaction, possibly including major cooperative investments, cannot equate to the intensity of relationships implied by *living together in a village*, while groups of agriculturalists, occasionally aggregating to undertake a project and celebrate rituals, can do so. We do not deny the importance of the sociality created by monuments, but we reject the need to say that it makes people resemble us in the same way that living in a village supposedly does.

Symbolic and religious revolutions

Related to the proposed cognitive revolution, and arising directly from the increase in material symbolism which appears to occur around the start of the Neolithic, is an argument that sees the Neolithic Revolution as a fundamental change in the nature of symbolism and religious belief. We have tried to show that this increase in symbolism is part of a very long-term process, and that, as can readily be observed, the rapid increase in materialism happens alongside sedentism, suggesting that the practicalities of portability may well have been an operative factor (another indication that the so-called cognitive and religious revolutions may have a taphonomic aspect). However, a number of scholars, notably Jacques Cauvin in 2000, have claimed that there is a change in the type and meaning of symbolism – not just in its frequency. Lewis-Williams and Pearce (2005: 59) see this as cosmology being 're-evaluated, refashioned and brought into line with a new social dispensation'.

Cauvin's influential model is perhaps most neatly summed up in the title of his book, translated into English as 'The birth of the gods and the origins of agriculture' – which leaves no room for doubt about the nature of the change he saw. Cauvin's symbolic revolution is not just about quantity. He thinks rather that it marks the appearance of ideas of anthropogenic supernatural beings – gods. He argues that earlier Palaeolithic Venus figurines are in some way just fertility symbols, but with agriculture the figure becomes 'truly a goddess' (p. 29). He supports his case by pointing out that there are images where other anthropomorphic figures are seen in apparent supplication to a god figure. He has no doubt about this interpretation, and sees that it is at this moment (he says around 9500 BC) that the evidence suggests that what is emerging is 'so close to that of the great historical religions that will follow ... [that] it is as if we were in some sort discovering their origin' (p. 71). People in the process of changing their economy, and settling down, recognize both the power of a god and their own limitations. Cauvin argues that the emergence of divinity in human form is central to the neolithization process and the accelerating pace of change. The central place given to an anthropomorphic god principle is a key part of the revolution – part of the process of alienating and externalizing the natural world, which many see as making a fundamental difference between hunter-gatherers and farmers. Lewis-Williams and Pearce make similar arguments, relating changes in cosmology and religion at this time to the changing character and rise of hierarchy (e.g. Lewis-Williams and Pearce 2005: 81). They develop the distinction between hunter-gatherers being in nature and farmers controlling nature by arguing that Neolithic communities in southwest Asia used architecture to create replica cosmoses: 'in doing so they gained greater *control* over the cosmos, and were able to adjust beliefs about it to suit social and personal needs' (p. 85). This is argued to be central to the Neolithic revolution:

5. The Neolithic mind

> Therein lies the real, innovative essence of the Neolithic:
> expression of religious cosmological concepts in material
> structures as well as in myths, rather than the passive
> acceptance of natural phenomena (such as caves), opened
> up new ways of constructing an intrinsically dynamic
> society. (2005: 167)

Hunter-gatherers passively accept the cosmological world as
given: farmers, on the other hand, control it, dynamically driving forward.

If this were correct, it would be an extremely powerful claim,
justifying the notion of revolution, and indicating a major
break with the past, when people's world views changed.
Barker (2006) appears to accept that there is a major change in
belief systems, which he describes as a shift to theism, and
though he does not devote much space to this change, he
observes that it is a common theme around the world. Since
Cauvin introduced his idea, substantial new lines of evidence
have emerged, especially the development of special-purpose
buildings during the PPNA, and the possible appearance of
ritual centres, such as Gobekli Tepe (Schmidt 2001) or Kfar
HaHoresh (Goring-Morris 2000).

This hypothesis therefore clearly requires careful examination. Cauvin (2000) and Watkins (2004) have both suggested
that while we can appreciate the aesthetic qualities of Palaeolithic art, and realize that it has ritual and religious meaning,
we cannot understand it. Cauvin stresses that there are no
gods in the Palaeolithic. In contrast to this he suggests that we
can readily understand Neolithic art, not just superficially but
at a more sophisticated level. Talking about the 'mother goddess' he says that 'The ambiguity of the symbol ... is readily
decipherable for us who bear the "terrible" mother in the deep-
est stratum of our unconsciousness' (Cauvin 2000: 71). What is
more, according to Cauvin in Neolithic religion we can see the
origin of the mother goddess who dominated Oriental pan-
theons until the time of the male-dominated pantheon of Israel,
as well as the origin of the Minoan bull contest, and even the

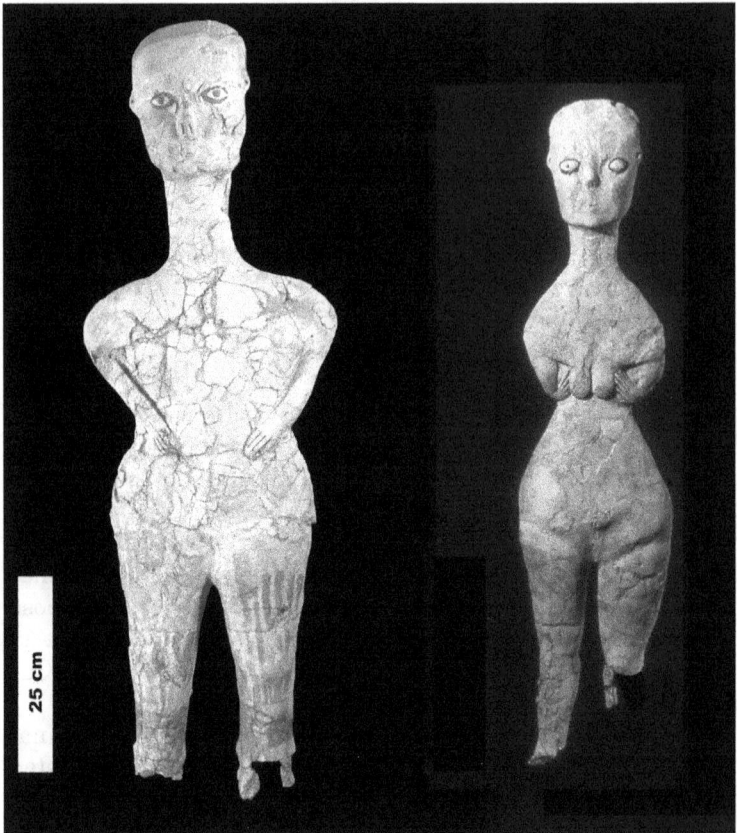

14. Plaster statues from 'Ain Ghazal, Jordan, Middle PPNB. The statue on the right is unusual in that the gender is clearly shown.

origin of sacred theatre. He does accept that there are a few problems; for example he does not consider the 'Ain Ghazal statues to be very beautiful (see Fig. 14), and believes his opinion is valid because other PPNB sculptors (his example is from Jericho) could produce works of talent (but see Rollefson 2001 for a different viewpoint). This view comes out again in Cauvin's statement about the burial of modelled skulls, where he assumes that these must be ancestors who have fallen out of favour, as it 'makes no sense at all for a skull that is buried'

112

5. The Neolithic mind

(Cauvin 2000: 114). These highly subjective value judgements of prehistoric art and its purpose can only be accepted if we believe that the Neolithic was on course to become Western civilization, and that its iconography and belief systems are comprehensible in light of these later developments.

We can of course argue the contrary. In a sense the extraordinary figures from 'Ain Ghazal make it very clear that PPNB artwork has a ritual context, and that we need to be very careful about assuming that we really comprehend PPNB religion. Kuijt (2000b) has looked at the patterns of skulls, and has suggested that there is a magical quality to their burial and caching, with regular repetition of the number three, or multiples of three. Lewis-Williams and Pearce (2005) argue that the use of shells for eyes replicates the blank stare of humans in trance states, and references altered states of being. Here we see hints at an entirely specific, historical sets of meanings. It is hard to get beyond just noting that there are patterns, but we can see that it is not all direct and simple figurative meaning.

This becomes extremely important for our comprehension of art and symbols if we hold that one of the most significant changes occurring at this time was in the use of symbols in materialization. It seems to be very clear that in the twenty-first century we tend to latch on to naturalistic art and the monumental. The carved, naturalistic animals of the northern Levant, especially those on the enigmatic 'T'-shaped pillars found in rings at Gobekli Tepe (see Fig. 15), are generally preferred to the abstract patterns or the eerie plaster statues of the southern Levant. The symbolic revolution appears to diminish in importance as it almost comes to seem that it is more about how much naturalistic art we can recognize, or how many animal species we can see carved. The naturalistic aspects of Upper Palaeolithic cave art in northern Spain and southern France allowed them to be interpreted as indications of a universal human trend to naturalistic representation, even if, in some instances, the pictures are demonstrably highly encoded, non-naturalistic narratives. Returning to the consideration of ritual and religion in the Levant, we find at the same

113

time, as we so often do in other forms of evidence, that the supposedly evolutionary trend is all wrong. Strangely, although houses themselves may become more elaborate as time goes on, as for example at Çatalhöyük, the ritual centres and buildings – even communal buildings of any sort – seem to disappear, not to reappear until we get the even more spectacular temples of Telailat Ghassul (Bourke 2001). The general assumption behind much of this story is once again based on analogy. Hunter-gatherers are shamanistic, animalistic, part of the natural world. Farmers are theists, removed from the world, and somehow this gives them an agency role and permits change. In many instances the analytical focus is heavily on the farmers, and not the preceding hunter-gatherers: Lewis-Williams & Pearce note the difficulty of reconstructing belief systems for the Upper Palaeolithic and Mesolithic, but ultimately fall back on fragments and generalizations, frequently stressing 'caves'. Thus, the ritualized uses of the 'deep limestone caves' of France and Cantabria are seen as a link to the cosmology of Upper Palaeolithic hunter-gatherers in the Near East, despite 'geographical distance and a general absence of deep caves in the Near East' (2005: 82). As so often, the hunter-gatherer appears to be a blank slate against which we can model our Neolithic selves.

If we accept the thesis that the origins of religion are to be associated with the development of farming, then we accept a major division of the world into these two categories of people. We have already argued extensively against such a black-and-white division, and do not see art or ritual as providing conclusive evidence for it. To claim that they do appears to depend on a circular argument. To begin with, Cauvin had to dismiss the Palaeolithic Venus figurines, and decide that they were not anthropomorphic gods. His reasoning is not at all clear. Simply announcing that the earlier figurines are fertility symbols, while the later ones are proper goddesses, is not convincing. Hunter-gatherer world views cannot simply be dismissed as simple and primitive. The rich belief system of the Australian Aboriginals has been described as one of 'the most

15. Monumental early Neolithic structures at Gobekli Tepe, Turkey.

coherent, or perhaps more precisely the most *structurally evolved*, the world has yet seen' (Barnard 1999: 60). We also note that recent accounts by David Lewis-Williams of the symbolic meanings of Upper Palaeolithic art and Neolithic ritual (Lewis-Williams 2002, Lewis-Williams & Pearce 2005) suggest that both are founded on similar principles of organization of the human brain.

Barker says that 'the long process of domestication was as much about people taming their fears of the dangers associated with death, reproduction, and sexuality as about taming nature (2006: 410) and thereby asserting 'the primacy of humans over the natural world' (p. 414). There seems to be some uncertainty as to whether these were fears that people had always had, or newly arose out of an attempt to control the world, or whether they are simply our fears. Cauvin is clear that these developments began before agriculture, questioning the close association ascribed to them, while, as argued above, Lewis-Williams sees symbolic domestication of animals happening long before herding began. If we accept Barnard's ideas of a hunter-gatherer mode of thought which generally outlasts any economic change, then perhaps we should also accept that the ideological changes, that occur long before farming had become the dominant subsistence economy, were ideologies that belonged to hunter-gatherers. As noted above, if people grow into their environment in the process of development, it seems unlikely that fear is a characteristic of their relationship with it. Many ethnographies of hunter-gatherers suggest a rich familiarity with all aspects of their environment and a thorough sense of being *at home* in the landscape.

Discussion

This chapter has focused on recent discussions of cognitive and symbolic revolutions that supposedly separate hunter-gatherers from farmers in the past. We have suggested that the cognitive arguments, though stimulating, are problematic in that they do not pay sufficient attention to the ways in which hunter-gatherers inhabit their landscapes and therefore may be confusing the appearance of evidence with the appearance of a revolution. The so-called religious revolution we find harder to assess, as its foundations appear to be built upon sand. Put simply, we find little concrete support for the dismissal of much evidence that hunter-gatherer belief was 'religious' and we note that different forms of belief (or 'consciousness contracts': Lewis-Williams & Pearce 2005) will characterize different cultures and that these may have different levels of archaeological visibility.

The implication of the claims that it is only with the Neolithic revolution that people become humans, is that pre-Neolithic hunter-gatherers are not human; indeed, if correct, it leaves the humanity of contemporary hunter-gatherers open to some question. For this latter group, it is not sufficient to imply that later interactions between hunter-gatherers and farmers lead to changes. Either the particular conditions of the Neolithic revolution in all of its geographical manifestations lead to cognitive change or they do not – the attempt to have things both ways removes any explanatory force that the evidence might supply. In a twenty-first-century, post-colonial context, we find it a startling proposition that hunter-gatherers are not human in the same way as farmers. Of course, it replicates the 'farmers equal us', 'hunter-gatherers equal other' distinctions which, as we have tried to show, underlie many uses of these categories. If the Neolithic revolution is understood as a fundamental disjuncture in human history, then the process of crossing the boundary, and the relations between those who have crossed it and those who have not, become of critical interest. We examine this debatable point in our final chapter.

6

Constructing histories

Should hunter-gatherer studies be transformed into a
contemporary history of people with a hunter-gatherer
background or, to put it more cautiously, a contemporary
history of people who (or whose ancestors) used to be
classified as hunter-gatherers? (Widlok 2004: 217)

Our discussions have demonstrated the ways in which views
about the essential characteristics of hunter-gatherers and
farmers, and about possible revolutions between them, have
always been highly coloured by modern political relationships,
and can lead to sharp divisions among those who study them.
In contrast, giving more attention to the great variety of human social organization in the past and present allows for fresh
narratives to be constructed about historical change. These
histories are more local, and more specific in character, and
these features make for some tension with the broad scale of
many accounts that emphasize revolution. They require close
engagement with the evidence, and the realization that contemporary, often romanticized, models of hunter-gatherers or
farmers do not make simple analogues for the societies of the
transitional periods. All this, of course, is not to deny the
importance of large-scale change, but it is to argue that our
understandings of it must be constructed with more subtlety
than some models allow. Here we examine some evidence of
transitions to agriculture in Europe, focusing on what we see as
the creative interplay of different traditions in bringing about
new ways of life. We then examine how a label such as 'Neolithic' cuts across a more dynamic spectrum of change. Finally,

we look at how local detail and long-term narrative may be integrated in considering the origins of agriculture.

Transitions in middle and western Europe

By the mid-Holocene, northwest Europe was populated by a diverse range of hunter-gatherers. Some of these are described by archaeologists as 'complex', others appear to have manifested little in the way of material inequality or permanent settlement. These hunter-gatherers then came into contact with a new way of life, farming. The adoption of agriculture in Europe was not an indigenous transition, in the sense of local domestication events. Crops and animals were, in the main, introduced to the area. Debate about the nature of the transition has concentrated on the processes by which farming interacted with hunting and gathering, and has often been polarized between proponents of an indigenous adoption of the idea of agriculture and those who believe that the main historical trajectory was the colonization of new lands by expanding farming groups. Even without revisiting these debates, the transition to agriculture in Europe provides further evidence of the complexity of relationships between hunter-gatherers and farmers over space and time. This evidence gives support to our contention that the distinction between the two life-styles cannot be seen as a fundamental disjuncture, but that the transition was made in a context in which varied forms of human society were generated. Perhaps it was even one in which we can talk of an 'evolution of evolvability' (see Introduction).

One of the most striking features of the Neolithization of central Europe is the rapid appearance of *Linearbandkeramik* (LBK) groups in the mid-eighth millennium (calibrated years BP). Named after their distinctive pottery style, the LBK groups appear as a rapid and major change in the archaeological records of the region. Their communities constructed large timber longhouses, often in clusters, sometimes enclosed, and frequently grouped together on high quality agricultural land. It is a form of architecture without previous local parallels.

119

Many archaeologists saw the appearance of LBK settlements as clear evidence of agricultural colonization – waves of farmers arriving from the east and displacing or replacing indigenous hunter-gatherer societies, which are often supposed to have been mobile, small scale, and historically rather insignificant. On the coasts of Europe, however, the hunter-gatherers persisted and from the mid-eighth millennium BP to *c*. 6000 years BP groups of hunter-gatherers and farmers lived in adjacent areas.

The rapid LBK expansion has been tied into broader models of the transition, notably the 'wave of advance' proposed by Ammerman and Cavalli-Sforza (1973). This model argued that population growth among farmers led to 'demic diffusion', whereby excess population generated by farming societies moved into low population areas immediately adjacent to their homes, having little interaction with the indigenes. A model was constructed for the coastal areas that provided for a greater degree of interaction between the different groups. The rapid expansion of the LBK thus came to be presented as a classic example of agricultural colonization; with new populations moving into hunter-gatherer lands. We might see these agriculturalists as radically different people, separated from the hunter-gatherers they encountered by a key historical progression.

More recently, however, many commentators have concluded that the LBK phenomenon resulted from the interplay of indigenous communities and new arrivals. Several strands of evidence have been significant, including continuities in stone tool traditions, and some evidence for the early appearance of ceramics and domesticated species among hunting and gathering communities in central Europe (for review, see Gronenborn 1999, 2007). Recent analysis of ancient DNA has been used to argue that early agriculturalists 'had limited success in leaving a genetic mark on the female lineages of modern Europeans' (Haak *et al.* 2005: 1017).

Further work on LBK skeletal remains from the cemeteries of Flomborn and Schwetzingen suggests that mobility of differing kinds between groups of people was very important. A high proportion of the burials at Flomborn, a very early LBK cemetery, were not of men and women who grew up in the area, suggesting, possibly, that the first farmers had migrated into this area. At the later cemetery of Schwetzingen a significantly smaller proportion of the population were migrants, and most of these were young women. One interpretation of this finding is that these women were marrying into the farming community, either from other farming groups or from hunter-gatherer ones. Some analysts have combined skeletal and other archaeological data to discuss the specialization of individual households within larger communities (Bentley 2007), and evidence on this point has led some commentators to describe a situation where 'male and female members of local pastoralist and/or hunter-gatherer communities lived side-by-side with members of immigrant farming societies (immigrants from Transdanubia and southwestern Slovakia) in multitraditional communities, which only at a coarse archaeological resolution appear to be LBK villages' (Burger *et al.* 2006: 1875). Rather than implying a meeting of humans of radically different and incompatible kinds, this suggests that while varied groups of people carried out varied economic practices, this did not stop them forming distinctively new kinds of communities.

In some places, then, hunter-gatherers and farmers in Europe appear to have interacted and formed new types of community and social organization rapidly. But these were not the only ways in which the technology of agriculture moved. On the Mediterranean coast of southern France, for example, recent evidence suggests that the first appearance of agriculture resulted from colonization, *c.* 7800-7600 calibrated years BP, by very small groups of farmers from Italy (Guilaine & Manen 2007). Interaction between these farmers and the local hunter-gatherers then led to the creation of a new archaeological entity (the 'Cardial', named after distinctively decorated pottery). This in turn then spread into other parts of France and the Iberian peninsula. It is especially interesting to note that the rapid expansion of the new agricultural technologies and associated material goods comes after an initial phase of small-scale contact. It is important to be clear here that this is not a delay caused by population levels, but a time during which new forms of organization are being created. Again, the impression is not of hunter-gatherers and farmers living in distinct worlds, but of communities working out new ways of relating to each other. This, of course, is nothing more nor less than the processes of interaction between different groups that had happened throughout the Mesolithic in Europe – the difference this time simply being that one group happened to be farmers.

Labelling the Neolithic

Archaeological terms frequently serve as labels, whose definition may shift and change over time. Probably this observation is nowhere more significant than in its application to the term 'Neolithic'. Originally developed as a term in the subdivision of the European Three Age system of Stone, Bronze and Iron, the Neolithic (or New Stone Age) was defined by John Lubbock in 1868, on the basis of material culture. It referred to the period of polished stone tools, as distinct from the Palaeolithic (or Old Stone Age). The rest of the package of things that belong in the Neolithic, such as pottery, gradually took shape. It was not until the twentieth century that the economic basis for the identification of the Neolithic began to take over. Given the comprehensive nature of the relevant economic change, its slow association with the coming of the Neolithic as defined by material culture is interesting. The terminology developed for northwest Europe was subsequently transferred to southwest Asia as prehistoric archaeological field work began to be conducted there. At this point the idea of the Neolithic hit problems. The package that had been seen as having been introduced into Europe as whole, did not seem to appear synchronously in this other environment. During her excavations at Jericho, Kathleen Kenyon developed the idea of a 'Pre-Pottery Neolithic' to account for the phases in which it appeared that farming had developed while pottery was absent. The association of pottery with farmers has subsequently been further eroded, most notably by the very early Jomon pottery of Japan, produced by hunter-gatherers. This lack of synchronicity for the package at the start of the Neolithic has since become notorious, as our knowledge has developed, and we can now see much earlier antecedents for many Neolithic traits, while in southwest Asia the earliest Neolithic and the latest Epipalaeolithic become harder to separate.

In attempts to redefine the Neolithic, there are scholars who would put the PPNA with the Epipalaeolithic rather than the Neolithic, and others who would draw the boundary within the PPNA, basing their definition on the emergence of 'village society' (Byrd 2005), and correlating this with a poorly defined late PPNA stage. An equally good case could surely be made that throughout the PPN the so-called Neolithic package was still developing and coming together, and that it is not until the Pottery Neolithic that we can really see that everything is in place. Inevitably, however, we do not in fact have to wait until the Pottery Neolithic to see pottery in southwest Asia – it appears within what is still labelled the PPNB as classified by other criteria. If we accept that our archaeological stages are being marked by a more nuanced covariation of a number of traits, rather than being simply defined by key fossil artefact types, we may see that we are now employing a more sophisticated label. However, such an approach equally serves to stress how frequently traits develop at different rates, and rather than producing more sharply defined periods, this lack of synchronicity may serve to blur their edges. Such a recognition immediately changes our attitude to change over time and to revolutions.

Despite his interest in symbolism and religion, Cauvin stressed, in a debate with his translator, that for him the Neolithic is defined by subsistence production. He says: 'Neolithic man is therefore "Neolithic" in the sense that he is the first human producer and that there was no other before him' (2000: 207), although he does recognize that others use the idea of village culture, which allows a Neolithic to be defined where some villagers are living on wild resources. Some writers have adopted the use of 'Neolithic' in discussing a process of neolithization (Gebel 2004), allowing the inclusion of early developments and a very long time-scale, running from within the Epipalaeolithic to at least the end of the PPNB, and therefore precluding the 'revolutionary' concept. This use of Neolithic as process essentially relies heavily on the idea of progress in a certain direction, towards the development of a specific package that we can see with hindsight to have been important for the agricultural underpinning of Western civilization. We have already discussed the flaws in such an approach, but here we wish to address a somewhat different point.

As far as defining the Neolithic is concerned, we are still stuck in an overall framework that privileges certain traits, the ones that we see as having later importance. Whether we refer to villages, crops, or gods, the model requires a big and dramatic change to have happened, and that this change should have taken place over a short enough period for it to be really noticeable. Unfortunately, adopting this as the starting point, rather than working from our evidence, leads to the classificatory problem described above, where we know something important happened, but we aren't sure what it was, and therefore cannot say when it happened. Rather than revolutions we might do better to think of *tipping points* (cf. Gamble 2007) – points at which developments that have long been evolving become truly significant.

The importance of the tipping point is in the change having accumulated, rather than representing a sudden shift. There is evidence for a long and slow development of symbolic material culture, from the Middle Palaeolithic's relatively slight remains, to Upper Palaeolithic art, both cave and mobile, and through the Epipalaeolithic to Natufian art. We can identify various diversifications and specializations in subsistence, including everything from specialized hunting in the Upper Palaeolithic, to the cereals harvested at Ohalo II. In this sense there is relatively little that we could call 'revolutionary' in the

124

Neolithic, and you could argue for different Neolithic start dates, depending on which trait you choose. This leads to an additional problem, that the process does not happen either at a uniform pace throughout the region, nor at key foci, but as a patchwork of development in many smaller provinces. Alongside tipping points there is the important issue of unintended consequences. Decisions made for one immediate reason may have severely limited any later possibilities for variation, or they may have led to paths being taken that were entirely unimagined.

Long sequences, local narratives

If we understand the Neolithic to be simply part of a continuous history of change, with processes that have no fixed point of origin, but which gradually come more and more into focus through the occasional moments of preservation afforded us by archaeology, then we have to accept that there is no real beginning, no simple 'origin' for the Neolithic as a whole. The economic and social flexibility that appears to be a hallmark of contemporary hunter-gatherer societies and of the Natufian (as exemplified by Early, Late, Final and Harifian), is perhaps one of the most important features that develops through the Upper and Epipalaeolithic sequence. In terms of tipping points, it may be significant that investment in specialized ways of life, such as permanent sedentism, and plant and animal domestication, starts to reduce flexibility and diversity. These innovations are coupled with new social arrangements, and with population densities that in some ecological areas can be sustained by no other means than by intensifying the exploitation of resources within one area. In that sense, the way of life reproduced by modern hunter-gatherers probably does share much with ancient hunter-gatherers. However, sharing flexibility and diversity does not provide much of a basis for assuming common behaviour, rather it reminds us that these behaviour patterns are diverse. What is more, they are not solely the preserve of hunter-gatherers. There are also farming societies that manage to maintain this flexibility, where populations do not become so dense that they cannot periodically revert to hunting and gathering. Indeed, the histories of some contemporary hunter-gatherer groups shows that this path has been taken many times.

Against this background, it becomes important to identify the particular tipping points, the points of no return, that mark specific local histories. The tipping point that may have prevented a return to hunting and gathering in the Levant may well have occurred late in the sequence of events; much later than sometimes supposed. It appears that in the Late PPNB there was still considerable flexibility and change, with the early development of pastoralism and the ending of the large settlements (or 'megasite' form). The proportion of wild resources to cultivated ones continues to decline. Interestingly, within the Pottery Neolithic we really begin to see a new form of landscape developing, a hierarchical one, where there are small settlements devoted to farming, which gradually begin to feed into larger ones, which in turn begin to acquire new functions. By the Bronze Age the hierarchy of settlements included real urban centres at the top. For the people involved there is clearly no turning back to a hunting and gathering option without a radical restructuring of society and economy. We are beginning to understand that there were other small settlements associated with the megasites in the PPNB, but they do not appear to have operated in a hierarchical fashion. Rather, we see desert seasonal animal exploitation sites, such as those reported by Sumio Fujii in the Jafr basin (Fujii 2007) as being the direct continuance of special-purpose camps surrounding a base camp.

New ways of life like these appear to have developed in the course of the Upper Palaeolithic. It seems relatively easy therefore to dismiss any idea of a revolution at the start of some not yet defined moment in the Neolithic. There remains the question 'why did foragers become farmers?', the subtitle of Barker's recent synthesis, *The Agricultural Revolution in Prehistory* (2006). Barker notes that it is not really until the 1960s that people really wondered why foragers had become farmers. Before then either the benefits of farming or the natural human evolutionary trajectory had seemed sufficient explanation. Doubts arose partly from the new understanding of hunter-gatherers and their affluent society. The economic ideas associated with the new concepts of 'man the hunter' and the 'new archaeology' led to an understanding that the transition was a long process, pushed and pulled by various factors, and that the Neolithic was an almost accidental tipping point, when people had moved the balance of their economy to the point where it was impossible not to become farmers. Underlying this perception there was still the notion of a one-way evolutionary path. Barker (p. 38) turns to cognitive changes to mark the separation: 'There is no doubt that there are profound differences between the "world-views" of foragers and non-industrial farmers today ... prehistoric foragers and farmers are likely to have been somewhat similarly differentiated in how they viewed the world and their sense of place within it.'

One of the points we have tried to make in this book is that an approach such as Barker's still depends on a categorization and a distinction that are largely artificial, and the product of modern Western values. As he himself says (p. 40), 'one of the most surprising aspects of the history of the debate has been how often sophisticated arguments have continued to be structured implicitly around a notion of an inevitable progression (and indeed progress) from foraging to farming as an unstoppable one-way historical process'. We agree entirely that this does still seem to underlie much work. A rare exception is Rowley-Conwy (2001), who provides examples of past hunter-gatherer societies which appear to become complex but return to simplicity, and who notes that, especially for the examples in the Arctic, no one would ever suggest that they are *en route* to agriculture.

It is not surprising that the changes happened at different rates and in different ways. However, this returns us to the question of covariance, the idea of a package of traits forming the Neolithic, and to debates on whether the Neolithic was

primarily a social or an economic change. It would be foolish to
attempt to deny that society and economy were not closely
entwined, but one message that appears to emerge in the
regions we are considering – and the pattern would only be
amplified if we attempted to look elsewhere in the world – is
that covariance is remarkably weak. If we were to consider, for
example, the pattern of sedentism, we would note that there
were some limited signs of increasing sedentism in the early
Natufian, a decline in the late and final Natufian and a major
increase during the PPNA, all within what can only be seen as
essentially hunter-gatherer economies. Then there is a substantial increase in sedentism and scale of community during
the PPNB which, just as the economy is really beginning to be
something we could describe as agricultural, finally goes
through a major phase of settlement collapse. It would appear
that neither is society driving the economy, nor vice versa.

One of the difficulties in looking for a universal model to
explain the transition to farming around the world is that it
necessarily removes all context from the process. Even within
the portion of the Old World that we have been looking at,
there is enormous variation, and not just between our two
major provinces of Europe and southwest Asia. The thousands
of years that separate different transitional processes may
appear close in terms of a hominid-scale past, but they are not
so strikingly close in the smaller-scale shorter history of the
Upper Palaeolithic and modern humans. There are substantial, enormous differences, in terms of the history of people.
Taking a bottom-up, local history approach, however, allows us
to consider what actually appears to be happening, in all of its
richly varied detail. It also allows us to consider the roles of
people and of the agencies at work in the process. In these
ways, the localized approach emphasizes the variability of the
human past. The adoption of agriculture was not part of an
inevitable evolutionary sequence, nor an accidental economic
slide, but a result of choices, actions and negotiations, with
some of the greatest unintended consequences ever seen.

Discussion

Our contention is that archaeological approaches to change in the past have tended to focus on step-like changes between periods, or other analytical constructs, and that as a consequence, models of revolutionary change have been made plausible. All histories run the risk of teleology, and this is particularly important in considering those that purport to explain the origins of the modern world. The development of agriculture in prehistory was demonstrably of key significance, but some modern accounts of this innovation have been problematic. We have pointed out that the concepts of both hunter-gatherer and farmer are rather more complex than is sometimes supposed, and moreover, that these concepts can be demonstrated to have played a key role in the construction of modern political identities. When they are imported uncritically into narratives of revolutionary change, the powerful oppositions such as 'them' to 'us', 'within nature' to 'outside of nature', 'historically important' to 'marginal', are enormously problematic for analysis. We have suggested that the use of these terms actively reduces our understanding of past variability, and that it may simply reproduce the modern world in the past. This is not to argue against the use of carefully founded analogy, but only to suggest that our concepts and labels require considerable care and precision in their use.

Most of the changes supposedly associated with a Neolithic revolution – the first villages, the first inequality – can also be demonstrated to be problematic. We would contend also that many of the broader claims for change – in cognition, religion, and possibly even in the nature of our humanity – are not well founded. In all of these cases, we would suppose that rather than search for a mythical origin point (and actually basing it on a simplistic stereotype of modern hunter-gatherers) we should look much more critically at particular historical conditions and consider the full range of variability in human lifestyles that is presented by the archaeological record.

To our minds, the aim of archaeology is to explain human

change over the long term, recognizing that past forms of human organization are likely to be much more diverse than those existing today. We have suggested that it is imperative that we continue to concentrate on the long term, but to recognize that different trajectories characterize different aspects of our evidence, and that the use of blanket labels for the totality is not helpful. Instead, by considering a mosaic of different interactions within and between communities, and in a variety of media, we arrive at a different vision of how change originated. Change was real, and as in any form of evolution, it was often unidirectional. Once a choice is made, it can be very difficult to turn back. Agriculture, as we recognize it now, is the result of a process of individual choices, from the first realization that a plant provided a reliable food stuff and the decision to utilize that resource heavily, right through to the processes (both deliberate and accidental) involved in the domestication of that particular species and its final integration into a broader package of agriculture. It is likely that there was a multitude of tipping points in this concatenation of decisions. Understanding them requires a commitment to human histories, in all of their messy local and complex manifestations.

References

Akkermans, P.M.M.G., Cappers, R., Cavallo, C., Nieuwenhuyse, O., Nilhamn, B. & Otte, I. (2006) 'Investigating the early pottery neolithic of northern Syria: new evidence from Tell Sabi Abyad', *American Journal of Archaeology* 110/1, 123-56.

Ammerman, A.J. & Cavalli-Sforza, L.L. (1973) 'A population model for the diffusion of early farming in Europe', in C. Renfrew (ed.) *The Explanation of Culture Change*, 345-57 (London: Duckworth).

Anderson, D.A. (2006) 'Dwellings, storage and summer site structure among Siberian Orochen Evenkis: hunter-gatherer vernacular architecture under post-Socialist conditions', *Norwegian Archaeological Review* 39, 1-26.

Ashcroft, B. & Ahluwalia, P. (1999) *Edward Said: The Paradox of Identity* (London: Routledge).

Aurenche, O. & Kozlowski, S.K. (1999) *La naissance du Néolithique au Proche-Orient ou le paradis perdu* (Paris: Editions Errance).

Banning, T. (2001) 'Settlement and economy in Wadi Ziqlab during the Late Neolithic', in *Jordan by the Millennia: Studies in the History and Archaeology of Jordan* 7, 149-55 (Amman: Department of Antiquities of Jordan).

Barker, G. (2006) *The Agricultural Revolution in Prehistory: Why Did Foragers Become Farmers?* (Oxford: Oxford University Press).

Barnard, A. (1999) 'Modern hunter-gatherers and early symbolic culture', in R. Dunbar, C. Knight & C. Power (eds) *The Evolution of Culture*, 50-68 (Edinburgh: Edinburgh University Press).

Barnard, A. (2004) 'Hunting-and-gathering society: an eighteenth century Scottish invention', in A. Barnard (ed.) *Hunter-Gatherers in History, Archaeology and Anthropology*, 31-43 (Oxford: Berg).

Barton, C.M., Ullah, I. & Mitasova, H. (2010). 'Computational modeling and socioecological dynamics: a case study from southwest Asia', *American Antiquity* 75(2), 364-86.

Bar-Yosef, O. (1998) 'The Natufian culture in the Levant, threshold to the origins of agriculture', *Evolutionary Anthropology* 6/5, 159-77.

Belfer-Cohen, A. & Bar-Yosef, O. (2000) 'Early sedentism in the Near East. A bumpy ride to village life', in I. Kuijt (ed.) *Life in Neolithic Farming Communities: Social Organization, Identity and Differentiation*, 19-37 (Kluwer Academic/Plenum Press: New York).

References

Bentley, A. (2007) 'Mobility, specialisation and community diversity in the linearbandkeramik: isotopic evidence from the skeletons', in A. Whittle & V. Cummings (eds) *Going Over: The Mesolithic-Neolithic Transition in North-West Europe*, 117-40 (London: British Academy).

Binford, L.R. (1980) 'Willow smoke and dog's tails: hunter-gatherer settlement systems and archaeological site formation', *American Antiquity* 45(1), 4-20.

Binford, L.R. (2001) *Constructing Frames of Reference: An Analytical Method for Archaeological Theory Building Using Ethnographic Data Sets* (Berkley: University of California Press).

Bird-David, N. (1990) 'The giving environment: another perspective on the economic system of gatherer-hunters', *Current Anthropology* 31, 189-96.

Bird-David, N. (1999) 'Introduction: South Asia', in R.B. Lee & R. Daly (eds) *The Cambridge Encyclopaedia of Hunters and Gatherers*, 231-7 (Cambridge: Cambridge University Press).

Bogaard, A. (2005) ' "Garden agriculture" and the nature of early farming in Europe and the Near East', *World Archaeology* 37(2), 177-96.

Bogaard, A. & Isaakidou, V. (2010) 'From megasites to farmsteads: community size, ideology and the nature of early farming landscapes in Western Asia and Europe', in B. Finlayson & G.M. Warren (eds) *Landscapes in Transition*, 192-207 (Oxford: Oxbow, CBRL Monograph).

Bourke, S. (2001) 'The Chalcolithic Period', in B. MacDonald, R. Adams & P. Bienkowski (eds), *The Archaeology of Jordan*, Sheffield: Sheffield Academic Press, 2001, pp.107-162.

Brody, H. (2001) *The Other Side of Eden: Hunter-Gatherers, Farming and the Shaping of the World* (London: Faber & Faber).

Brophy, K. (2007) 'From big house to cult house: early Neolithic timber halls in Scotland', *Proceedings of the Prehistoric Society* 73, 75-96.

Burger, J. et al. (2006) 'Response to comment on "Ancient DNA from the first European farmers in 7500-year-old Neolithic sites" ', *Science* 312(5782), 1875.

Byrd, B. (2005) 'Reassessing the emergence of village life in the Near East', *Journal of Archaeological Research* 13.3, 231-90.

Caulfield, S. (1978) 'Neolithic fields: the Irish evidence', in H.C. Bowen & P.J. Fowler (eds) *Early Land Allotment in the British Isles: A Survey of Recent Work*, 137-43 (Oxford: British Archaeological Reports British Series 48).

Caulfield, S. (1983) 'The Neolithic settlement of North Connaught', in T. Reeves-Smyth & F. Hamond (eds) *Landscape Archaeology in Ireland*, 195-216 (Oxford: British Archaeological Reports British Series 116).

Caulfield, S., O'Donnell, R.G. & Mitchell, P.I.. (1998) ' ^{14}C dating of a Neolithic field system at Céide Fields, County Mayo, Ireland', *Radiocarbon* 40, 629-40.

Cauvin, J. (1987) 'L'apparition des premières divinités', *La Recherche* 18/194, 1472-80.

References

Cauvin, J. (2000) *The Birth of the Gods and the Origins of Agriculture* (Cambridge: Cambridge University Press).

Chaix, L., Bridault, A. & Picavet, R. (1997) 'A tamed brown bear (*Ursus arctos L.*) of the Late Mesolithic from La Grande-Rivoire (Isère, France)?', *Journal of Archaeological Science* 24(12), 1067-74.

Cheney, D.L. & Seyfarth, R.M. (2007) *Baboon Metaphysics: The Evolution of a Social Mind* (London: University of Chicago Press).

Childe, V.G. (1964) *What Happened in History* (Harmondsworth: Penguin).

Cooney, G. (2000) *Landscapes of Neolithic Ireland* (London: Routledge).

Cummings, V. (2003) 'The origins of monumentality? Mesolithic world views of the landscape in western Britain', in L. Larsson, H. Kindgren, K. Knutsson, D. Loeffler & A. Åkerlund (eds) *Mesolithic on the Move: Papers Presented at the Sixth International Conference on the Mesolithic in Europe, Stockholm 2000*, 74-80 (Oxford: Oxbow).

Cummings, V. (2010) 'Formalising the sacred? The late Mesolithic and early Neolithic monumental landscapes of Britain and Ireland', in B. Finlayson & G.M. Warren (eds) *Landscapes in Transition*, 115-24 (Oxford: Oxbow, CBRL Monograph).

Dahlberg, F. (1983) *Woman the Gatherer* (Yale University Press).

Delage, C. (2004) 'Beyond past cultural geography: example of the Levantine late epipaleolithic', in C. Delage (ed.) *The Last Hunter-gatherers in the Near East*, 95-117 (Oxford: British Archaeological Report International Series 1320).

Descola, P. (2005) *Par-delà nature et culture* (Paris: CNRF Gallimard).

Donald, M. (1991). *Origins of the Human Mind: Three Stages in the Evolution of Culture and Cognition* (Cambridge: Harvard University Press).

Ellen, R. (1982) *Environment, Subsistence and System: The Ecology of Small-scale Social Formations* (Cambridge: Cambridge University Press).

Endicott, K.L. (1999) 'Gender relations in hunter-gatherer societies', in R.B. Lee & R. Daly (eds) *The Cambridge Encyclopaedia of Hunter-Gatherers*, 411-18 (Cambridge: Cambridge University Press).

Evans, E.E. (1966) *Prehistoric and Early Christian Ireland: A Guide* (London: Batsford).

Fabian, J. (1983) *Time and the Other: How Anthropology Makes its Object* (New York, Columbia).

Ferriter, D. (2005) *The Transformation of Ireland 1900-2000* (London: Profile).

Finkel, M. (2009) 'The Hadza', *National Geographic*, December 2009 http://ngm.nationalgeographic.com/2009/12/hadza/finkel-text (accessed 3 March 2010).

Finlayson, B. & Mithen, S. (2007) *The Early Prehistory of Wadi Faynan, Southern Jordan, Archaeological Survey of Wadis Faynan, Ghuwayr*

References

and al-Bustan and Evaluation of the Pre-Pottery Neolithic A Site of WF16 (Oxford: Wadi Faynan Series vol. 1, Levant Supplementary Series vol. 4, CBRL and Oxbow Books).

Ford, R.I. (1985) 'The processes of plant production in prehistoric North America', in R.I. Ford (ed.) *Prehistoric Food Production in North America*, 1-18 (Ann Arbor: University of Michigan Press).

Foster, R.F. (2001) *The Irish Story: Telling Tales and Making it up in Ireland* (London: Penguin).

Fowler, C.S. & Turner, N.J. (1999) 'Ecological/cosmological knowledge and land management among hunter-gatherers', in R.B. Lee & R. Daly (eds) *The Cambridge Encyclopaedia of Hunters and Gatherers*, 419-25 (Cambridge: Cambridge University Press).

Freeman, M. (2004) *Victorians and the Prehistoric: Tracks to a Lost World* (London: Yale).

Frick, F.S. (1997) 'Cities', in E.M. Myers (ed.), *The Oxford Encyclopedia of Archaeology in the Near East* 1: 14-19 (Oxford: Oxford University Press).

Fujii, S. (2007) 'PPNB barrage systems at Wadi Abu Tulayha and Wadi Ar-Ruwayshid Ash-Sharqi: a preliminary report of the 2006 Spring field season of the Jafr Basin Prehistoric Project, Phase 2', *Annual of the Department of Antiquities of Jordan* 51, 403-27.

Gamble, C. (2007) *Origins and Revolutions: Human Identity in Earliest Prehistory* (Cambridge, Cambridge University Press).

Garfinkel, Y. (2004) *The Goddess of Sha'ar Hagolan. Excavations at a Neolithic Site in Israel* (Jerusalem: Israel Exploration Society).

Gebel, H.G. (2004) 'There was no center: the polycentric evolution of the Near Eastern Neolithic', *Neo-Lithics* 1/04: 28-32.

Goring-Morris, A.N. (1987) *At the Edge: Terminal Pleistocene Hunter-Gatherers in the Negev and Sinai* (Oxford: British Archaeological Reports International Series 361(i)).

Goring-Morris, A.N. (2000) 'The quick and the dead: the social context of aceramic Neolithic mortuary practices as seen from Kfar Hahoresh', in I. Kuijt (ed.) *Life in Neolithic Farming Communities: Social Organization, Identity and Differentiation*, 103-36 (New York: Kluwer Academic/Plenum Publishers).

Gould, J.R. & Gould, C.G. (2007) *Animal Architects: Building and the Evolution of Intelligence* (New York: Basic Books).

Gould, S.J. & Vrba, E.S. (1982) 'Exaptation: a missing term in the science of form', *Palaeobiology* 8: 4-15.

Gronenborn, D. (1999) 'A variation on a basic theme: the transition to farming in Southern Central Europe', *Journal of World Prehistory* 13: 123-210.

Gronenborn, D. (2007) 'Beyond the models: "Neolithisation" in Central Europe', in A. Whittle & V. Cummings (eds) *Going Over: The Mesolithic-Neolithic Transition in North-West Europe*, 73-98 (London: British Academy).

References

Guenther, M. (1999) 'From totemism to shamanism: hunter-gatherer contributions to world mythology and spirituality', in R. Lee & R. Daly (eds) *The Cambridge Encyclopaedia of Hunters and Gatherers*, 426-33 (Cambridge: Cambridge University Press).

Guenther, M. (2007) 'Current issues and future directions in hunter-gatherer studies', *Anthropos* 102, 371-88.

Guilaine, J. & Manen, C. (2007) 'From Mesolithic to Early Neolithic in the Western Mediterranean', in A. Whittle & V. Cummings (eds) *Going Over: The Mesolithic-Neolithic Transition in North-West Europe*, 21-51 (London: British Academy).

Gurven, M. & Hill, K. (2009) 'Why do men hunt: a reevaluation of "man the hunter" and the sexual division of labour', *Current Anthropology* 50(1), 51-74.

Haak, W. *et al.* (2005) 'Ancient DNA from the first European farmers in 7500-year-old Neolithic sites', *Science* 310(5750), 1016-18.

Harris, D.R. (1989) 'An evolutionary continuum of people-plant interaction', in D.R. Harris & G.C. Hillman (eds) *Foraging and Farming: The Evolution of Plant Exploitation*, 11-26 (London: Unwin).

Harris, D.R. (1996) 'Domesticatory relationships of people, plants and animals', in R. Ellen & K. Fukui (eds) *Redefining Nature: Ecology, Culture and Domestication*, 437-63 (Oxford: Berg).

Harris, D.R. (2007) 'Agriculture, cultivation and domestication: exploring the conceptual framework of early food production', in T. Denham, J. Iriarte & L. Vrydaghs (eds) *Rethinking Agriculture*, 16-35 (Walnut Creek: Left Coast Press, One World Archaeology Series).

Herity, M. & Eogan, G. (1977) *Ireland in Prehistory* (London: Routledge).

Hodder, I. (1990) *The Domestication of Europe: Structure and Contingency in Neolithic Societies* (Oxford: Blackwell).

Hodder, I. (2005) 'Changing entanglements and temporalities', in I. Hodder (ed.) *Changing Materialities at Çatalhöyük*, 1-22 (Cambridge: Macdonald Institute Monographs).

Ingold, T. (1999) 'On the social relations of the hunter-gatherer band', in R. Lee & R. Daly (eds) *The Cambridge Encyclopaedia of Hunters and Gatherers*, 399-410 (Cambridge: Cambridge University Press).

Ingold, T. (2000) *The Perception of the Environment: Essays in Livelihood, Dwelling and Skill* (London: Routledge).

Kelly, R.L. (1995) *The Foraging Spectrum: Diversity in Hunter-gatherer Lifeways* (London: Smithsonian Institute Press).

Kinzel, M. (2006) 'The architectural reconstruction', in H.G.K. Gebel, H.J. Nissen & Z. Zaid, *Basta II: The Architecture and Stratigraphy*, 181-202 (Berlin: *ex oriente*).

Köhler-Rollefson, I. & Rollefson, G.O. (1990) 'The impact of Neolithic man on the environment: the case of 'Ain Ghazal, Jordan', in S. Bottema, G. Entjes-Nieborg & W. van Zeist (eds) *Man's Role in the Shaping of the Eastern Mediterranean Landscape*, 3-14 (Rotterdam: Balkema).

References

Krech III, S. (1999) *The Ecological Indian: Myth and History* (London: W.W. Norton & Co).

Kuijt, I. (2000a) 'When the walls came down: social organization, ideology and the "collapse" of the pre-Pottery Neolithic', in H.G. Gebel & H.D. Bienert (eds) *Proceedings of the Symposium on Central Settlements in Neolithic Jordan: Studies in Early Near Eastern Production, Subsistence and Environment*, vol. 5 (Berlin: *ex oriente*).

Kuijt, I. (2000b) 'Keeping the peace. Ritual, skull caching, and community integration in the Levantine Neolithic', in I. Kuijt (ed.) *Life in Neolithic Farming Communities: Social Organization, Identity and Differentiation*, 137-64 (New York: Kluwer Academic/Plenum Press).

Kuijt, I., Finlayson, B. & MacKay, J. (2007) 'Pottery Neolithic landscape modification at Dhra' ', *Antiquity* 81: 106-18.

Larsson, L. (1990) 'Dogs in fraction: symbols in action', in P. Vermeersch & P. Van Peer (eds) *Contributions to the Mesolithic in Europe*, 153-60 (Leuven: Leuven University Press).

Layton, R.H. (2001) 'Hunter-gatherers, their neighbours and the nation state', in C. Panter-Brick, R. Layton & P. Rowley-Conwy (eds) *Hunter-gatherers: An Interdisciplinary Perspective*, 292-321 (Cambridge: Cambridge University Press).

Lee, R. & Daly, R. (1999) 'Introduction: foragers and others', in R. Lee & R. Daly (eds) *The Cambridge Encyclopaedia of Hunters and Gatherers*, 1-19 (Cambridge: Cambridge University Press).

Lee, R. & Daly, R. (eds) (1999) *The Cambridge Encyclopaedia of Hunters and Gatherers* (Cambridge: Cambridge University Press).

Lee, R.B. (1988) 'Reflections on primitive communism', in T. Ingold, D. Riches & J. Woodburn (eds) *Hunter-Gatherers, History, Evolution and Social Change*, 252-68 (Oxford: Berg).

Lee, R.B. & DeVore, I. (eds) (1968) *Man the Hunter* (New York: Aldine).

Lewis-Williams, D. (2002) *The Mind in the Cave: Consciousness and the Origins of Art* (London: Thames & Hudson).

Lewis-Williams, D. & Pearce, D. (2005) *Inside the Neolithic Mind: Consciousness, Cosmos and the Realm of the Gods* (London: Thames & Hudson).

Macalister, R.A.S. (1928) *The Archaeology of Ireland*, 1st edn (London: Methuen).

Macalister, R.A.S. (1935) *Ancient Ireland: A Study in the Lessons of Archaeology and History* (London: Methuen).

Macalister, R.A.S. (1949) *The Archaeology of Ireland*. 2nd edn (London: Methuen).

MacLaughlin, J. (1995) *Travellers and Ireland: Whose Country, Whose History?* (Cork: Cork University Press).

McCall, G.S. (2007) 'Add shamans and stir? A critical review of the shamanism model of forager rock art production', *Journal of Anthropological Archaeology* 26(2), 224-33.

References

McCarter, S.F. (2007) *Neolithic* (London: Routledge).

McDonagh, M. (1994) 'Nomadism in Irish Travellers' identity', in M. McCann, S. Ó Síocháin & J. Ruane (eds) *Irish Travellers: Culture and Ethnicity*, 95-109 (Belfast: Queens University for Anthropological Association of Ireland).

McGhee, R. (2004) *The Last Imaginary Place: A Human History of the Arctic World* (Toronto: Key Porter Books/Canadian Museum of Civilization).

McMillan, A.D. & Yellowhorn, E. (2004) *First Peoples in Canada* (Toronto: Douglas & McIntyre).

Mellars, P. (1976) 'Fire ecology, animal populations and man: a study of some ecological relationships in prehistory', *Proceedings of the Prehistoric Society* 42: 15-45.

Midgley, M. (2002) *Evolution as a Religion*, revised edn (London: Routledge).

Mitchell, G.F. (1956) 'An early kitchen-midden at Sutton, Co. Dublin', *Journal of the Royal Society of Antiquaries of Ireland* 86, 1-26.

Moore, A.M.T., Hillman, G.C. & Legge, A.J. (2000) *Village on the Euphrates* (Oxford: Oxford University Press).

Morgan, L.L.D. 1877 *Ancient Society* (London: Macmillan).

Murray, H.K., Murray, J.C. & Fraser, S.M. (eds) (2009) *A Tale of the Unknown Unknowns: A Mesolithic Pit Alignment and a Neolithic Timber Hall at Warren Field, Crathes, Aberdeenshire* (Oxford: Oxbow).

Nadel, D. (2004) 'Wild barley harvesting, fishing, and year-round occupation at Ohalo II (19.5 KY, Jordan Valley, Israel)', in Le Secrétariat du Congrès (ed.) *Acts of the XIVth UISSP Congress, University of Liege (September 2001): Section 6: The Upper Palaeolithic (General Sessions and Posters)*, 135-43 (Oxford: British Archaeological Report International Series 1240).

Özdogan, M. (1997) 'Anatolia from the last glacial maximum to the Holocene climatic optimum: cultural formations and the impact of the environmental setting', *Paléorient* 23/2, 249-62.

Olszewski, D.I. (1991) 'Social complexity in the Natufian? Assessing the relationship of ideas and data', in G.A. Clark (ed.) *Perspectives on the Past: Theoretical Biases in Mediterranean Hunter-gatherer Research*, 322-40 (Philadelphia: University of Pennsylvania Press).

Panter-Brick, C., Layton, R.H. & Rowley-Conwy, P. (2001) 'Lines of enquiry', in C. Panter-Brick, R.H. Layton & P. Rowley-Conwy (eds) *Hunter-gatherers: An Interdisciplinary Perspective*, 1-11 (Cambridge: Cambridge University Press).

Peterken, G.F. (1996) *Natural Woodland: Ecology and Conservation in Northern Temperate Regions* (Cambridge: Cambridge University Press).

Pluciennik, M. (2004) 'The meaning of 'hunter-gatherers' and modes of subsistence: a comparative historical perspective', in A. Barnard (ed.)

References

Hunter-Gatherers in History, Archaeology and Anthropology,17-29 (Oxford: Berg).

Pluciennik, M. (2005) *Social Evolution* (London: Duckworth).

Pollan, M. (2006) *The Omnivore's Dilemma: A Natural History of Four Meals* (London: Penguin).

Price, T.D. & Brown, J.A. (eds) (1985) *Prehistoric Hunter-gatherers: The Emergence of Cultural Complexity* (Orlando: Academic Press).

Price, T.D. & Gebauer, A. (1995) 'New perspectives on the transition to agriculture', in T.D. Price & A. Gebauer (eds) *Last Hunters, First Farmers: New Perspectives on the Prehistoric Transition to Agriculture*, 3-20 (Santa Fe, NM: School of American Research Press).

Quintero, L.A. & Wilke, P.J. (1995) 'Evolution and economic significance of naviform core-and-blade technology in the Southern Levant', *Paléorient* 21(1): 17-33.

Renfrew, C. (2003) *Figuring it out* (London: Thames & Hudson).

Renfrew, C. (2007) *Prehistory: The Making of the Human Mind* (London, Weidenfeld & Nicolson).

Rindos, D. (1984) *The Origins of Agriculture: An Evolutionary Perspective* (Orlando: Academic Press).

Rollefson, G.O. (1997) 'Changes in architecture and social organisation at 'Ain Ghazal', in H.G. Gebel, Z. Kafafai & G.O. Rollefson (eds) *The Prehistory of Jordan II: Perspectives from 1997*, 287-308 (Berlin: *ex oriente*).

Rollefson, G.O. (1998) 'Neolithic 'Ain Ghazal: ritual and ceremony III', *Paléorient* 24(1): 45-58.

Rollefson, G.O. (2001) '2001: an archaeological Odyssey', *Cambridge Archaeological Journal* 11(1): 112-14.

Rollefson, G.O. & Gebel, H.G. (2004) 'Towards new frameworks: supraregional concepts in near eastern neolithization', *Neo-Lithics* 1/04: 21-2.

Roscoe, P. (2009) 'On the "pacification" of the European Neolithic: ethnographic analogy and the neglect of history', *World Archaeology* 41(4), 578-88.

Rowley-Conwy, P. (2001) 'Time, change and the archaeology of hunter-gatherers: how original is the "original affluent society"?', in C. Panter-Brick, R. Layton & P. Rowley-Conwy (eds) *Hunter-gatherers: An Interdisciplinary Perspective*, 39-72 (Cambridge: Cambridge University Press).

Sahlins, M.D. (1972) *Stone Age Economics* (Chicago: Aldine).

Said, E.W. (1978) *Orientalism: Western Conceptions of the Orient* (London: Penguin).

Schmidt, K. (2001) 'Göbekli Tepe, Southeastern Turkey. A preliminary report on the 1995-1999 excavations', *Paléorient* 26/1, 45-54.

Schweitzer, P. (2001) 'Silence and other misunderstandings: Russian anthropology, Western hunter-gatherer debates, and Siberian peoples', in P. Schweitzer, M. Biesele & R. Hitchcock (eds) *Hunters and Gatherers*

References

in the Modern World: Conflict, Resistance, and Self-Determination, 29-51 (Oxford: Berghahn).

Service, E.R. (1962) *Primitive Social Organisation* (New York: Random House).

Sharples, N. (2000) 'Antlers and Orcadian rituals: an ambiguous role for red deer in the Neolithic', in A Ritchie (ed.) *Neolithic Orkney in its European Context*, 107-16 (Cambridge: McDonald Institute Monographs).

Shott, M.J. (1992) 'On recent trends in the anthropology of foragers. Kalahari revisionism and its archaeological implications', *Man* 27: 843-71.

Simmons, A. & Najjar, M. (2004) 'Ghuwayr I, a pre-pottery Neolithic B settlement in southern Jordan: report of the 1996-2000 campaigns', *Annual of the Department of Antiquities of Jordan* 47, 407-30.

Smail, D.L. (2007) *On Deep History and the Brain* (London: University of California Press).

Smith, B.D. (2001) 'Low-level food production', *Journal of Archaeological Research* 9: 1-43.

Smyth, J. (2006) 'The role of the house in early Neolithic Ireland', *European Journal of Archaeology* 9(2/3), 229-57.

Smyth, J. (2010) 'The house and group identity in the Irish Neolithic', *Proceedings of the Royal Irish Academy* 110C, 1-29.

Sollas, W. (1911) *Ancient Hunters and their Modern Representatives* (London: Macmillan & Co.).

Spriggs, M. (2008) 'Ethnographic parallels and the denial of history', *World Archaeology* 40(4), 538-52.

Sterelny, K. & Griffiths, P.E. (1999) *Sex and Death: An Introduction to the Philosophy of Biology* (London: University of Chicago Press).

Taçon, P.S.C. (1991) 'The power of stone: symbolic aspects of stone use and tool development in Western Arnhem Land, Australia', *Antiquity* 65, 192-207.

Tilley, C. (1996) *An Ethnography of the Neolithic* (Cambridge: Cambridge University Press).

Vrydaghs, L. & Denham, T. (2007) 'Rethinking agriculture: introductory thoughts', in T. Denham, J. Iriarte & L. Vrydaghs (eds) *Rethinking Agriculture*, 1-15 (Walnut Creek: Left Coast Press, One World Archaeology Series).

Waddell, J. (1998) *The Prehistoric Archaeology of Ireland* (Bray, Wordwell).

Warburton, D.A. (2004) 'Towards new frameworks: supra-regional concepts in near eastern neolithization', *Paléorient* 30/1, 183-8.

Warren, G.M. (2007) 'Mesolithic myths', in V. Cummings & A. Whittle (eds) *Going Over: The Mesolithic-Neolithic Transition in North-West Europe*, 311-28 (London: British Academy).

Watkins, T. (1997) 'The human environment', *Paléorient*, 23/2, 263-70.

Watkins, T. (2004) 'Architecture and "theatres of memory" in the Neolithic

References

of Southwest Asia', in E. DeMarrais, C. Gosden & C. Renfrew (eds) *Rethinking Materiality: The Engagement of Mind with the Material World*, 97-106 (Cambridge: McDonald Institute Monographs).

Watkins, T. (2005) 'The Neolithic Revolution and the emergence of humanity: a cognitive approach to the first comprehensive world view', in J. Clarke (ed.) *Archaeological Perspectives on the Transmission and Transformation of Culture in the Eastern Mediterranean*, 84-8 (Oxford: CBRL and Oxbow, Levant Supplementary Series 2).

Watkins, T. (2009) 'Ordering time and space: creating a cultural world', in M.M.J. Córdoba, C. Pérez, I. Rubio & S. Martínez (eds) *5th International Congress on the Archaeology of the Ancient Near East*, 647-59 (Madrid: Universidad Autónoma de Madrid).

Widlok, T. (2004) '(Re-)current doubts on hunter-gatherer studies as contemporary history' in A. Barnard (ed.) *Hunter-gatherers in History, Archaeology and Anthropology*, 217-26 (Oxford: Berg).

Wilmsen, E.N. (1983) 'The ecology of illusion: anthropological foraging in the Kalahari', *Reviews in Anthropology* 10/1, 9-20.

Wilson, P.J. (1988) *The Domestication of the Human Species* (New Haven: Yale University Press).

Woodburn, J. (1982) 'Egalitarian societies', *Man* 17, 431-51.

Woodman, P.C., McCarthy, M. & Monaghan, N. (1997) 'The Irish quaternary fauna project', *Quaternary Science Reviews* 16, 129-59.

Zvelebil, M. (2008) 'Innovating hunter-gatherers: the Mesolithic in the Baltic', in G. Bailey & P. Spikins (eds) *Mesolithic Europe*, 18-59 (Cambridge: Cambridge University Press).

Index

Index

Index

Index

www.ingramcontent.com/pod-product-compliance
Lightning Source LLC
Chambersburg PA
CBHW062040270326
41929CB00014B/2482